Praise f

"This wonderfully insightful book has challenged me to think more deeply about what is required of us, individually and collectively, as we struggle to face the challenges presented by our racial history with greater courage, compassion, and creativity. I'll be contemplating this guidance—and putting some of it into practice—in the months and years to come."

MICHELLE ALEXANDER
author of *The New Jim Crow:
Mass Incarceration in the Age of Colorblindness*

"This powerful and penetrating book offers us healing medicine for the great suffering of racism. Ruth King, a deeply wise and caring meditation teacher and diversity consultant, not only helps us understand the complexity of our great racial divide, she offers a core of practices, reflections, and actions that gives us hope for transformation. Our world needs this book. We need this book. Please read with a receptive heart and share with all you know!"

TARA BRACH
author of *Radical Acceptance* and *True Refuge*

"It is not possible to have justice without healing the body that has experienced injustice. And it is not possible to heal without transforming this unjust system. In *Mindful of Race*, King explores the impact of racial injustice on communities at the margins. She further illustrates practices black people can embody to support our longevity and dignity. This book belongs in the hands of every activist—regardless of race! We need to develop a new language, a language that centers healing and restoration."

PATRISSE CULLORS
cofounder of Black Lives Matter and
author of *When They Call You a Terrorist*

"In *Mindful of Race*, Ruth King accomplishes a rare feat: she offers us an incredibly accessible, relatable, and useful guide for addressing the range of ways we internalize racist messages. She also beautifully lays out the common thoughts and feelings that function—despite our best intentions—to protect rather than ameliorate racism. In doing so, she has made engaging with this text a deeply affective, as well as intellectual, experience. Perhaps most importantly, King addresses the emotional and spiritual impacts of racism that are so rarely addressed in workshops and textbooks but that are critical to our collective and personal healing. King includes reflection exercises and discussion questions, making this a very useful guide for a range of settings. *Mindful of Race* is a brilliant and unique addition to the struggle for racial justice."

ROBIN DIANGELO, PHD
author of *White Fragility: Why It's So Hard for White People to Talk About Racism*

"*Mindful of Race* is an important addition to the growing body of literature black Americans in the 21st century are publishing to create a bridge between East and West and heal generational racial suffering for all of humanity. King's approach is revolutionary in the deepest sense because it addresses our racial problems at their root, which is consciousness or the mind itself. *Mindful of Race* is rich in anecdotes and examples that will, I believe, cause a reader to smile and perhaps even say, 'Thank you.' *Mindful of Race* is a trustworthy guide for claiming our birthright—happiness and freedom."

CHARLES JOHNSON, PHD
author of *Middle Passage* and *Taming the Ox: Buddhist Stories and Reflections on Politics, Race, Culture, and Spiritual Practice*

"In her outstanding new book *Mindful of Race*, Ruth King explores the role of mindfulness in understanding the suffering of racism and the power of mindfulness for healing that corrosive conditioning. This is an arena of profound challenges, and her many years of meditative practice provide a depth of insight and wisdom that illuminates the work we all must do. *Mindful of Race* is a wonderfully pragmatic and inspiring guide on this journey of transformation. Highly recommended."

JOSEPH GOLDSTEIN
author of *Mindfulness: A Practical Guide to Awakening*

"This masterful and courageous book is a gift offered from the searing depths of America's ancestral racist wound. Its truth telling, both profoundly insightful and challenging with its compassionate means and liberating goals, makes *Mindful of Race* a clarifying and necessary addition to every home, school, and university curriculum. Ruth King's authentic writing invites us to meet her with vulnerability and honesty while at the same time inspiring us to faithfully engage the urgent task of accountability and racial healing. While having immediate appeal to those familiar with mindfulness, this highly practical book goes far beyond a clique audience. This is a book for everyone. Pick it up, read it, live with it, and share it on."

THANISSARA
author of *Time to Stand Up:
An Engaged Buddhist Manifesto for Our Earth*

"Important medicine, wise, heartfelt, both demanding and comforting. With many tools for the real work on racism we need in these polarized times."

JACK KORNFIELD
author of *A Path with Heart*

"Ruth King's work has had a positive impact on me personally and is highly influential in our community, Against the Stream Buddhist Meditation Society. As we all strive to end suffering and confusion, *Mindful of Race* is more than just a great book; it's a map to freedom."

NOAH LEVINE
author of *Dharma Punx* and *Against the Stream: A
Buddhist Manual for Spiritual Revolutionaries*

"*Mindful of Race* presents a remedy for the pain that has cut across us as human beings and has left a seemingly indelible scar upon our hearts. King boldly states that this mark can be dissolved! With great care, she carries us to the place in which we can rest and heal the racial divide."

ZENJU EARTHLYN MANUEL
author of *The Way of Tenderness: Awakening
through Race, Sexuality, and Gender*

"Acknowledging the prevailing wisdom of the past while building an enduring bridge to a new future, in *Mindful of Race* Ruth King invites us to discover and uncover the hurtful truth of our collective and chronic heart disease—racism. To be mindful of race day to day, minute to minute, gives us endless opportunity to pause, reflect, and then act in ways that heal and connect rather than harm and destroy. I wholeheartedly recommend you take this journey alone and together with others who truly want racism to end in our lifetime."

BARBARA E. RILEY, EDD
co-creator of Integral Matters™: Thriving on Difference
and author of *Are You Ready for Outrageous Success?*

"*Mindful of Race* is a breath of fresh air by which everyone can find a way to contribute to healing racial pain and divisiveness. By applying mindfulness practice to address racism, Ruth King provides one of the most exciting, hopeful, and useful applications of mindfulness for our times. The book shows how each of us can look within so that contributing to overcoming racism is not a burden; it is an expression of our compassion, wisdom, and mutual respect."

GIL FRONSDAL

author of *The Issue At Hand: Essays on Buddhist Mindfulness Practice*

"Powerfully relevant, timely, and accessible, Ruth King's *Mindful of Race* is a great contribution. She speaks from her wealth of experience to show how mindfulness and empathy can help us understand the effects of racism and move toward its ending. A must-read for everyone."

SHARON SALZBERG

author of *Lovingkindness* and *Real Love*

"In *Mindful of Race*, Ruth King boldly declares, 'Racism is a heart disease that's curable.' She then proceeds to guide us on a three-part journey to healing. In doing so, King brings all of her compassionate insight, talent, and grit to bear. This is a book for the ages, and it is exactly what the world needs now."

JAN WILLIS

author of *Dreaming Me: Black, Baptist and Buddhist—One Woman's Spiritual Journey*

"Ruth King brilliantly breaks down one of the most complex experiences of human suffering—racism and racial oppression—with the transformational life skills of mindfulness and Buddhist practice. Like the aspects of insight and concentration in meditation, she provides a laser focus in rebuilding our collective humanity using universal potentials of awareness and kindness in all of our hearts and minds. Ruth's book is a must-read, must-practice, must-live experience."

LARRY YANG

author of *Awakening Together*

MINDFUL

OF

RACE

Also by Ruth King

Healing Rage: Women Making Inner Peace Possible

Embracing the Mad Mind: Cultivating Calm in Chaos

The Emotional Wisdom Cards

Soothing the Inner Flames of Rage:
Meditations that Educate the Heart and Transform the Mind

MINDFUL

OF

RACE

Transforming
Racism
from the
Inside
Out

RUTH KING

SOUNDS TRUE
BOULDER, COLORADO

Sounds True
Boulder, CO 80306

Published 2018

Cover design by Lisa Kerans
Book design by Beth Skelley

Cover art by Lisa Kerans

Printed in Canada

Library of Congress Cataloging-in-Publication Data
Names: King, Ruth (Diversity Consultant), author.
Title: Mindful of race : transforming racism from the inside out / Ruth King.
Description: Boulder, CO : Sounds True, Inc., 2018.
Identifiers: LCCN 2017045105 (print) | LCCN 2018001540 (ebook) |
    ISBN 9781683640820 (ebook) | ISBN 9781683640813 (pbk.)
Subjects: LCSH: Racism–Religious aspects–Buddhism. | Spiritual
    life–Buddhism. | Attention–Religious aspects–Buddhism. |
    Awareness–Religious aspects–Buddhism.
Classification: LCC BQ4310 (ebook) | LCC BQ4310 .K56 2018 (print) |
    DDC 294.3/5675–dc23
LC record available at https://lccn.loc.gov/2017045105

10 9 8 7 6 5 4 3

For Barbara,
My beloved, my teacher, my friend

Contents

INTRODUCTION Racism Is a Heart Disease, and It's Curable! . . . 1

PART 1 **Understanding Habits of Harm— Diagnosis**

CHAPTER 1 Two Realities, One Truth . . . 17

CHAPTER 2 Individual and Group Racial Identity . . . 23

CHAPTER 3 Racial Group Dominance and Subordination . . . 35

CHAPTER 4 Six Hindrances to Racial Harmony . . . 45

Part 1 Summary . . . 69

PART 2 **Mindfulness—Heart Surgery**

CHAPTER 5 Life Is Not Personal, Permanent, or Perfect . . . 73

CHAPTER 6 Establishing a Daily Meditation Practice . . . 79

CHAPTER 7 Cultivating Calm: Sitting and Walking Practice . . . 83

CHAPTER 8 Kindness Practice . . . 93

CHAPTER 9 Understanding the Cycle of Misperception . . . 105

CHAPTER 10   Working with Racial Distress:
              RAIN Practice . . . 109

              Part 2 Summary . . . 127

PART 3   **Cultivating a Culture of Care—
          Recovery**

CHAPTER 11   Cultivating Moral Character . . . 131

CHAPTER 12   Compassion Practice . . . 145

CHAPTER 13   The Wake-Up Call: Racial Affinity Groups . . . 165

CHAPTER 14   Talking about What Disturbs You . . . 177

CHAPTER 15   What White People Can Do with Privilege . . . 189

CHAPTER 16   What People of Color Must Do Together . . . 213

CHAPTER 17   Artistry: Cultural Medicine . . . 237

CHAPTER 18   Equanimity Practice . . . 243

              Messy at Best! . . . 253

              Acknowledgments . . . 261

              About the Author . . . 265

Racism Is a Heart Disease, and It's Curable!

Something alarming happens when we think or hear the word *racism*. Something deep within us is awakened into fear. All of us, regardless of our race and our experience of race, get triggered, and more than the moment is at play. That word picks at an existential scab—some level of dis-ease at the mere insinuation of the word, some itch that we can't seem to scratch, or some fear we believe will harm us. This activation happens to all of us.

Regardless of how we look on the outside, we turn into frightened combatants and suit up for war. The heart quakes, and the mind narrows to its smallest, tightest place—survival. Whether or not we're conscious of it, we all tend to go to our weapons of choice—aggression, distraction, denial, doubt, worry, depression, or indifference. By virtue of a number of intersecting factors, including race, we carry with us varying levels of power to execute our desired outcome or to disguise our discomfort. Tension heightens, and the stress can feel intolerable—even life threatening. And for too many of us, such fear is not unfounded.

Some of us do not acknowledge that we are racial beings within the human race, nor do we recognize how or understand why our instinct as members of racial groups is to fear, hurt, or harm other races, including our own. And we don't know how to face into and own what we have co-created as humans. But each of us can and must ask ourselves two questions: Why are matters of race still of concern across the nation and throughout the world? And what does this have to do with me?

In the West, we live within a racial context of hatred and harm. Whether subtle or openly cruel, whether out of innocence or ignorance, the generational and often unconscious conditioning that has bred social and systemic norms of racial dominance, subordination, and separation, nuanced in every aspect of our day-to-day lives, is tightly sewn into the fabric of our society.

I'm writing this book in the year of the grand opening of the historic National Museum of African American History and Culture, part of the Smithsonian on the Washington Mall. Several months after it opened, a noose was found in front of a display titled, "Democracy Abroad. Injustice at Home." I'm writing on the fifteenth anniversary of the September 11 extremist attack on US soil. This same year, voters in Great Britain approved the Brexit referendum to exit the European Union, a decision driven not only by fear of being overrun by immigrants but also by a fear that globalization will undo long-established ways of life. The stunning Brexit vote was 52 percent to 48 percent.

I'm writing in the year Barack Obama, the first African American president of the United States, is ending his presidency, after enduring eight years of a horrific racist and obstructionist Republican Congress and Senate that, from the onset, proclaimed to ensure that Obama would fail and be a one-term president. Throughout his two-term presidency, blatant racism and relentless questioning and resistance to his leadership became the norm, all under the guise of governance.

I am writing in the heat of a human rights protest in the streets of Charlotte, North Carolina, where I live, after a police officer killed Keith Lamont Scott, a forty-three-year-old African American father of seven, who was in his car waiting to pick up his daughter from school. According to the Huffington Post, police killed more than 250 black people in 2016. That's about twenty-one black bodies per month or five per week.

In 2016, Republican candidate Donald Trump—who ran a racially charged and divisive presidential campaign of hate, fear, and prideful disrespect of women and dark-skinned bodies and immigrants—won the electoral vote. Now, in this era of Donald Trump, overt racism has been made entirely okay again in the halls of power. In the month following Trump's election, the Southern Poverty Law Center, which monitors hate groups and other extremist activity throughout the United States, reported 1,094 bias-related incidents across the nation.

As I write, Charlottesville, Virginia, has become ground zero for the Loyal White Knights of the Ku Klux Klan, who are protesting the city council's decision to remove a statue of Confederate General Robert E. Lee. This rally was considered the prerequisite of an alt-right march to be held a few weeks later. Alt-right marches are spreading across the nation and are not even denounced inside the Trump White House.

The long-standing demonization and criminalization of blacks and dark-skin bodies still occupy the psyches of the white people—mostly white men and the women who support them—who hold power in most US institutions.

On June 17, 2015, twenty-one-year-old Dylann Roof, a white male and Confederate loyalist, was welcomed into Emanuel African Methodist Episcopal Church in downtown historic Charleston, South Carolina—one of the oldest black churches in the United States and a site for community and civil rights organizing. Within an hour of being welcomed, during prayer, Roof gunned down and killed nine African Americans. The timing of these murders has significant historical relevance. In 1822, Denmark Vesey was suspected of planning a slave rebellion to take place in Charleston at midnight on June 16, 1822. When white citizens suspected this rebellion, thirty-five black people, including the church founder, were hanged, and the church was burned down.

The Charleston church shooting on June 17, 2015, occurred on the 193rd anniversary of this uprising.

The morning Roof was arrested—sixteen hours after being on the run and after admitting that he had hoped to ignite a race war—Roof complained of being hungry. John Ledford, a white police officer in Shelby, North Carolina, brought Roof food from Burger King and reported, "He was very quiet, very calm . . . . He was not problematic." *Not problematic?!* This is how racism works. A white man admits he wants to incite a race war, yet he is *not problematic*. A bit crazy, don't you think?

I'm writing this book at an intense time of global and civil wars: Wars against other nations and within nations. Wars against races, religions, and cultures. Greed wars on the youth, the elders, and the mentally and physically ill. Wars against the poor, against immigrants, against gays and transgendered people, and against women and girls. I'm writing at a time when the need for reform of criminal justice, economic justice, immigrant justice, LGBTQIA rights, and children's rights—to name a few—is clear. Race and racism are roots to these concerns. I am writing at a time of global fear—people fearing each other and the systems within which we exist. A time when greed is altering the planet that once sustained us, and the planet is revolting, as are its people, against exploitation and corruption.

The world's heart is on fire, and race is at its core. What's happening in the world today is the result of past actions. The bitter racial seeds from past beliefs and actions are blooming all around us, reflecting not only a division of the races that is rooted in ignorance and hate but also, and more sorely, a division of heart.

Racism is a heart disease. How we think and respond is at the core of racial suffering and racial healing. If we cannot think clearly and respond wisely, we will continue to damage the world's heart.

For well over twenty years, I've coached leaders and teams in cultivating cultures that are inclusive, creative, productive, and respectful. I was trained professionally in clinical psychology, organizational development, and diversity consulting, and this background supports me in seeing patterns of racial ignorance and distress that get in the way of us coexisting as humans. This background alone, however, while it brought awareness and understanding, did not transform my relationship to racial distress. The best tool I know of to transform our relationship to racial suffering is mindfulness meditation. For more than twenty years, that practice has supported me in experiencing racial distress without warring against it.

Mindfulness-based meditation has become vastly popular in modern-day secular life, being practiced in schools, prisons, hospitals, therapeutic programs, veteran centers, movement and other healing modalities, and corporations. It is also being studied scientifically. Mindfulness-based meditation is not a religious code as much as it is a social psychology that supports experiences of well-being. Research has shown it to have a positive impact on neurobiological functioning, stress reduction, and overall physical and mental well-being.

I was attracted to this practice because my habitual ways of relating to racial distress were not working. I was a righteous rager—I even wrote a book about rage—and I had many reasons to rage about race. But then, at the age of twenty-seven, I had open-heart surgery for a mitral valve prolapse, a surgical procedure that began a spiritual inquiry into my habits of harm. When introduced to mindfulness meditation years later, I learned how to interrupt the mental war I was inflicting on others and myself. I learned how to relate to distress with more compassion, and I opened to a deeper understanding of my racial conditioning. I discovered that how I thought was core not only to my level of distress but also to my ability to break habits of harm.

I have not reached nirvana, no. But I do know the freedom that comes from being able to look at what is happening—not what my mind is programmed to believe is happening, but what is really happening—without raging inside. Over time, this practice has profoundly impacted how I relate to both racial distress and racism in my relationships and communities. Through mindfulness meditation practice, I discovered the meaning of a quote often attributed to South African president Nelson Mandela: "When we can sit in the face of insanity or dislike and be free from the need to make it different, then we are free." That's what mindfulness meditation does. It helps us put a crucial pause between our instinctive and often overwhelming feelings of being wronged or harmed or in danger and our responses to those feelings. In that pause, we gain perspective—we find our breath, our heartbeat, and the ground beneath our feet. This, in time, supports us in seeing our choices more clearly and responding more wisely.

My journey of racial healing has been long, and it continues. A number of experiences converged to give birth to this book. My own mindfulness practice was revealing a deeper understanding of racial distress and increasing experiences of inner freedom. I was learning to sit with difficult feelings without coming apart, all the while growing in my capacity to look at what was happening within me as it was happening.

In 2008, the year President Obama was elected, I moved from a racially engaged and diverse community in Berkeley, California, to a racially segregated and cautious community in Charlotte, North Carolina. In Charlotte, I could feel, at my feet, the discontent of the ancestors and, at my face, a polite distance tinged with hostility.

Racial tension was at an all-time high following the killing of unarmed black men, women, and children by police, and there was civilian retaliation toward police officers. On one of my morning walks in Charlotte, I noticed that many of my neighbors, most of whom are white, had small US flags lining their yards in honor of the recently killed police officers. For years, I've walked this same path and never have I seen symbols of care for the masses of black lives who so viciously lost their lives at the hasty hands of police. I don't condone the killing of anyone, and I mean no disrespect to the vast territory of grief that engulfs us. Pain does not discriminate when it comes to senseless loss; it just hurts—it crushes our hearts. Yet, on this walk in my friendly neighborhood, I felt oddly diminished and felt compelled to make what is often invisible and glossed over more visible and pronounced.

Perhaps it's because my twenty-three-year-old grandson called me—distraught, in disbelief, and afraid—right after Alton Sterling's murder by police and just before Philando Castile's. Perhaps it's because my partner and I had been falling asleep crying in each other's arms, empty of words. Perhaps it's because the stories of our pain as a collective get broad brushed, easily forgotten, and buried in the criminality of our bodies. Perhaps it's because as a great-grandmother and elder, I can feel how endangered my children are as black bodies, and I can't guarantee them protection from harm.

My resettlement in the South has offered me innumerable opportunities for mindfulness practice, especially as I repeatedly replaced the missing Obama/Biden signs in my front yard. When I would get triggered by a remark, a conversation, a racist incident, or a terrible piece of racially charged news, I could take it to my meditation cushion and work through the feelings so that I could then think clearly enough to decide how I wanted to respond. What freedom that was—not to be held in the tight grip of anger, defensiveness, and fear; to be released from the bondage of being on red alert, always ready to have my rage engaged.

My other outlet was to sit and talk to my life partner, Dr. Barbara Riley, who has spent the bulk of her career working for racial justice. She and her colleagues have designed and developed an array of concepts, tools, and frameworks for transforming oppression, most notably Integral Matters™: Thriving on Difference. In our talks and walks, she shared her framework of understanding and working with racial issues as individuals, as members of identity groups, and within the institutions in which we work. It was through these talks that I realized the subtle depth of racial *group* identity and its contribution to structural racism. I have worked with this framework for several years integrating it with mindfulness principles, which is reflected in part 1 of this book.

Using my professional background in designing diversity leadership programs, along with my experience as a mindfulness practitioner and teacher, in 2010, I designed and began teaching the Mindful of Race program. This training brings a mindful inquiry to an examination of racial conditioning and social distress.

I was able to incorporate this training into multiyear programs in the Dedicated Practitioners Program and Community Dharma Leaders Program at Spirit Rock Meditation Center and in the Teacher Training Program at Insight Meditation Society, as well as the Meditation Teacher Training Institute of Washington, DC. In these programs, I was able to encourage an investigation of racial ignorance and social distress, which allowed me to witness the positive impact that examining race through the lens of mindfulness had on others over time. For the past several years, the Mindful of Race training has supported individuals and groups across the nation in understanding and transforming racial habits of harm. This book, to a large extent, grew from the soil of this program.

What you will find in this book comes not only out of my work as a meditation teacher, life coach, and diversity consultant but also from my personal experiences as an African American, married lesbian, and great-grandmother, raised with working-class values in South Central Los Angeles, in the heat of the civil rights and Black Power movements. I am not an expert at any of these identities, yet I speak through all of them. This book is also inspired by the countless people I have worked with over the years who are asking:

- How do I work with my thoughts, fears, and beliefs in ways that nurture the dignity of all races?

- How do I comfort my own raging heart in a sea of racial ignorance and violence?

- How can my actions reflect the world I want to live in and leave to future generations?

- How do I advocate for racial justice without causing harm and hate, internally and externally?

Racism is a heart disease. Many of us can live for a while with a heart disease without knowing it, and others of us know we have a heart disease but are afraid or even in denial about it. But racism is a heart disease, and it's curable! This book points us toward racial harmony and healing.

In part 1, Understanding Habits of Harm—Diagnosis, we discover the narrative we hold along racial lines—both conscious and unconscious. We examine our racial inheritance and habits and look at how social, historical, and cultural conditioning influences our perceptions and actions. We examine race through our individual and group identities and look at how dominant and subordinated group identities maintain racial ignorance, injustice, and the institutional proliferation of racism. This information supports us in clearly seeing our interdependence and the impact of our individual agency on collective and social well-being.

In part 2, Mindfulness—Heart Surgery, we explore how to stay present to racial distress through mindfulness meditation. We develop a mindfulness practice that can support us in investigating racial disease, while softening the grip of anger, guilt, and fear that arises when we do this work. This practice helps us experience the kinship, care, and relief that come from releasing racial distress. Through regular mindfulness practice, we begin to make peace with our own heart and mind and discover that, despite what is happening around us, we can recognize and discharge racial tension and distress within our body and mind and experience increasing moments of inner freedom.

A purely self-centered spiritual practice limits racial healing. Therefore, in part 3, Cultivating a Culture of Care—Recovery, we shift our focus outward. Using spiritual archetypes, we discover what it means to contribute to a culture of care with integrity, talk to our children about race, nurture racial literacy through racial affinity groups, talk about what disturbs us, develop the healing power of our creative expression, and discover the role of equanimity in social transformation.

Each of us has a racial story. While I can't know of your unique experiences as a racial being or of what you have experienced or escaped, what I do know is that if you are willing to take this journey with me, you will be able to recognize the shape of racial ignorance and suffering, find your part in it, and respond more wisely to change it.

A Few Biases and Caveats

To give this book the focus and shape it needs, I have had to isolate race, carving it out from the gestalt of social oppressions, all of which are worthy of attention and care. Racism, however, is the ism that I feel is the most insidious and the most enmeshed with our sense of social normalcy—and insanity. It's been discussed the longest, yet has not penetrated the global heart in ways that uproot its poisons. My wholehearted hope is that this book supports that uprooting.

In writing about racial conditioning and suffering, I am, of course, limited by my own experience, my language, and the problems inherent in categorizing complex experiences into small boxes. For example, I use many personal experiences, and I use the terms *blacks* and *African American* interchangeably. I have also lumped all people of color (POC) and all whites into equally small boxes, though I am well aware of the vast diversity that exists within each of these simplistic categories. I realize that by doing so, some people will feel that their experiences are not directly reflected here. However, speaking with such categorization affords me the opportunity to show racial habits of harm more pointedly.

I also recognize that the younger generations may have different experiences from those expressed here; they, therefore, may feel that this book does not speak to them. I understand that some biracial and multiracial people may struggle with picking sides and that some POC—Hispanics, Asians, dark-skinned immigrants, and many others—have experiences so painful that they too may feel underrepresented here. I acknowledge these differences and invite you to make connections to your specific experience by noticing the skeletal shape of oppression portrayed in this book.

I do not speak for all whites or all POC. And as just one African American woman, I don't represent the experiences of all African Americans. I still have much to learn about the complexity of racial group identities, which I feel is a gateway to understanding racial oppression. I want to further acknowledge that although I have traveled to many parts of the world, this book mostly speaks of race culture and slave mentality in the United States; thus, it may, at times, illustrate more black and white racial concerns that are foundational and unfinished within the United States. This book is in no way meant to shadow the sharp edge of racial oppression experienced by other races within the United States and throughout the world—including the indigenous peoples of the Americas and Africa, the aboriginal peoples of Australia and New Zealand, the Syrian and Palestinian people, and other people of dark skin, including Asian people who for generations have freely given Westerners like me the gift of the Buddha's teachings.

My fear of excluding any of us from this important and complex exploration or of simplifying any person's experience is one reason it has taken years to write this book. I have questioned myself, *Do I understand enough or know enough?* At some point, I realized that the answer was no—I didn't understand enough or know enough, but I would have to go ahead and write the book anyway. None of us knows enough, but we can't let that stop us. Despite the diversity of our experiences, what you will recognize on the following pages are the dynamics common among most oppressed groups and what sustains this dynamic.

And so, in this book, we will employ racial diversity and these gross categories of white and POC as a starting place, a point of entry. We will use them as a way to look closer, to look behind, beneath, and beyond the category to recognize how we relate to each other. And we will not stop there; we will open our eyes and hearts wider to see our humanity and to devote ourselves to ensuring social dignity and freedom for all.

My hope is to ignite your imagination and help you discover your voice in the song of racial healing. Together, we'll imagine the possibilities of who we could be and how we could live in this world if every one of us aimed our energy toward awakening, nonharming, generosity, and kinship—a world with race but without racism. It all begins with an examination of our habits of harm.

One last request: bring an ancestor with you. In the work of racial healing, we soon discover that we have inherited what's unfinished from our parents and ancestors. The meaning of our practice is deepened when we remember that we are not just doing this inquiry for ourselves. Bringing an ancestor with us can support our mindfulness of racial inquiry and healing.

Reflect for a moment: Is there someone in your bloodline whose relationship to race affected your life? Perhaps a keeper of the family history? Or someone who hated another race without apology? Or maybe there was a racial secret that was kept that everyone knew about but couldn't talk about. Maybe someone in your life left a mark on your heart and changed how you saw life—maybe a mind-set or view that you knew was wrong that you could not interrupt, or a view or belief that you knew was right but your efforts to nurture it were overpowered. Bring the threads of this racial legacy to mind so it can be seen clearly and be honored and transmuted through your awareness. Think about which ancestor you might want to bring along to transform the lineage business.

This book is a call to those who care deeply about racial harmony, people who want to go the distance by making a difference from the inside out. To begin, we must first take a deep breath and consent to this journey. We must be willing to be diligent in service to our belonging and to this planet that nurtures us. We must be willing to exchange comfort for racial consciousness and to be more curious than critical or dispirited.

If I didn't belong to you, I wouldn't have written this book. If you didn't belong to me, you wouldn't be reading it. I'm you, and you are me—you just don't know that yet. We are here, sharing these pages, to embrace our membership in each other's lives, to discover our wholeness, and to remember that we belong. Be willing to be a light and to let your heart lead the way.

Let's get on with it, shall we?

Part 1

UNDERSTANDING HABITS OF HARM

~ DIAGNOSIS ~

1

Two Realities, One Truth

A beautiful teaching often shared in Buddhist communities supports us in placing race in a social context. It's called the Two Truths Doctrine, and it describes two realities in which we all live: ultimate reality and relative reality. Simply stated, in relative reality, we are some bodies—formed, habituated, ego-driven, and relating to life through concepts. In ultimate reality, we are no bodies—formless, empty of self, and eternal. In relative reality, I am a woman, African American, lesbian, great-grandmother, artist, and elder. However, in ultimate reality, I'm none of these things. I am beyond conception; I am awareness dancing with the karmic rhythms of life.

In ultimate reality, there is neither race nor a reason to suffer. We are undivided and beyond definition. But in relative reality, we're all in considerable pain as racially diverse beings driven by fear, hatred, greed, and delusion.

In relative reality, language is commonly how we relate. Talking about race is messy because it brings to light our racial beliefs and values expressed in ignorance, innocence, and righteousness. Many of us show up with good intentions but are braced, bruised, and afraid. We put our foot in our mouth; we get scared, become frustrated or belligerent, or just shut down. We feel unclear, unskilled, angry, and cautious. Our mind plays habit songs that get in the way of our ability to connect and be open to what's right here. For example, the following comments are common narratives expressed from participants in the Mindful of Race training.

Whites commonly say

- I don't see color. Aren't we all the same?

- Race is an illusion. Why are POC so attached to this concept? Let it go!

- I'll just listen. I know I have a lot to learn. Besides, I'm likely to say something stupid and get nailed again.

- I don't know what I don't know. POC need to teach me about race; tell me what to do.

- Why are POC so angry with me? I wasn't living at the time.

- I don't know how to have this conversation without feeling blamed, guilty, frustrated, or angry.

- I'm oppressed in other ways, so I know what it feels like to be a POC.

- We can't really talk about race because there aren't enough POC in the room.

People of color commonly say

- Right, we're going to talk about race. This means that in addition to being disturbed by white people's ignorance, I'm going to have to teach white folks what they choose to deny knowing—amnesia of whiteness.

- I'm angry about race, but if I talk about it, I'm labeled the angry person, and nobody listens.

- Right, we're going to talk about race. That means we're going to talk about black folks and white folks. I'm neither! Why should I care? I'm invisible.

- Race is a concept. Why can't I just get over it?

- When will white people take responsibility for their collective impact on other races throughout the world?

- I don't want to keep educating white people about race. They need to do this for themselves.

- I don't need to be friends with white people. I just want them to stop getting in my way and stop doing harm.

- I'd like to be able to focus on something other than race for a change, but people who look like me keep getting harmed.

How did we get here? How do we understand these standoffs and this dread, even with people who willingly want to change? How do we transform these habits of harm that are common within relative reality? We can't heal if we can't talk to each other, and we can't talk to each other until we understand why we can't talk to each other.

While language and concepts are useful for organizing and navigating our relative or relational reality, we are also beyond concept. Ultimate reality is what we aspire to in spiritual practice—a felt sense of universal belonging, peace, and harmony that is beyond the limits of concept. Yet, at the core of racial suffering is a forgetting that we belong. Dr. Martin Luther King Jr. spoke of this eloquently:

> All life is interrelated, and we are all caught in an inescapable network of mutuality, tied in a single garment of destiny. . . . I can never be what I ought to be until you are what you ought to be. And you can never be what you ought to be until I am what I ought to be—this is the interrelated structure of reality.

This "interrelated structure of reality" points us toward the idea of ultimate reality or nonduality—our kinship in each other's lives. Yet we must first understand the ways in which we have been conditioned to relate to each other before we can know the true freedom of this wisdom. Race, in and of itself, is not as problematic as the meaning or the value we have historically placed on race and how this value impacts our direct experience with ultimate reality—that kinship of harmony.

It's easy to feel overwhelmed and discouraged by the repetitive motion of racial injury and injustice, yet there is no immediate outer solution. There is no getting around that fact that each of us is challenged with navigating the relative reality of race—the fact of these bodies in various shapes, colors, sizes, and experiences—so that we may know freedom. That freedom is our birthright—a freedom unconditioned, a peace we can know in the very midst of racial ignorance and distress.

Racial disease has to do with our histories, habits, and hearts. To understand racial habits of harm—the ways we avoid more genuine connection and healing as individuals and racial groups—is to dive below our knee-jerk responses, beneath the words themselves, to examine our conditioning. This requires us to work with our mind in order to transform our heart. We must be willing to be uncomfortable. In fact, we might consider discomfort a wake-up call inviting us to inspect the ways we have been programmed to blame or distrust each other and, in so doing, how we have learned to live with a heart disease.

Ultimate reality and relative reality are to be understood as two expressions of one truth, two sides of one coin. Ultimate reality is often associated with the ocean, and relative reality, with the waves; ultimate reality is like the sky, and relative reality is all that appears and disappears in the sky. Relative reality makes the knowing of ultimate reality possible, and we can't know ultimate reality outside of our bodily experiences.

We are made up of habit. We are all conditioned by each other in relative reality. The good news about habits is that, with awareness, they can change for the better. The following chapters are offered to help us understand the habits of mind that got us here and how we can get the blood circulating again through the heart of humanity.

2

Individual and Group Racial Identity

Racial identity is a dynamic part of relative reality. In this chapter, we explore our racial conditioning—how we were taught to belong to a particular race and to relate to racial "others." We will examine race and its power dynamics from two unique expressions: as individuals with diverse experiences and as members in racial group identities. We will also explore how our habits of mind are reflected in the world.

Parental Conditioning

From the beginning, our parents conceived our very being and gave us our names. We were held and shaped in the womb and made in the mold of our ancestors. We inherited our ancestors' DNA, and we were hardwired to their nervous system.

According to neuroscientist Dan Siegel, in his book *Mindsight: The New Science of Personal Transformation*, the autonomic nervous system—which regulates bodily functions that we are not conscious of, such as breathing, the heartbeat, and digestive processes—is older than our physical form:

> The nervous system begins in the embryo as the
> ectoderm; the outer layer of cells becomes the skin.
> Certain clusters of these outer cells then fold inward
> to form a neural tube—the spinal cord. . . . The whole

nervous system sets up its basic scaffolding, its core architecture, during development in the womb. Genetics are important for determining how neurons will migrate and then connect to each other.

We could say that the nervous system, the heart of relational well-being, is literally the skin that shapes and defines what we typically refer to as a self, hardwired with cellular memory. The very fibers of our being were passed down from our ancestors. In this sense, the regulation of bodily functions or impulses is, to some degree, preconditioned. Given the sensitive membrane that defines us, this gift from our ancestors, we can perhaps comprehend how intimately woven our nervous systems are to past and present conditioning, including racial conditioning. This may explain why we may feel anxious or frightened when we come into contact with certain races but can't readily explain why.

Our individual existence has also depended on food grown from the earth, water for bathing and drinking, sunshine and fire for warmth, and other bodies to know our own. We have been dependent on guidance, feedback, transport, and the actions of others to affirm us. We have been loved by nature, plants, animals, teachers, and strangers and supported by the fine minds of medicine, the skilled hands of healers, and, for many, the wisdom of spiritual guidance. We are not separate from our environment or the families we grew up in.

Our parents and their parents shaped our early views and beliefs. As children, our caregivers' expectations were programmed into our minds through reward and punishment. We learned to read body language and adapt to energy. As a result, we learned to perceive the world through our parents' image. Much of who we are—including our appearance, skin color, gestures, talents, habits, beliefs, and actions, as well as our relationship to our own race and to other races—is inherited from our parents and ancestors and is, without examination, passed on to the next generation.

On vacation recently in Cabo San Lucas, Mexico, an adolescent white boy was sitting on the beach with his father. The young boy and I had just purchased similar wristbands from a vendor, and I turned to him and said, "These are great, right?" The boy did not speak to me. Instead, he looked at his father as if to say, "I shouldn't speak, right?" The father didn't respond to his son, who was looking at him with tough-boy, yet pleading eyes. I, too, looked at his father expectantly when the boy didn't respond. The father then said to me unapologetically, "He doesn't like you." I said, "He doesn't know me." I could feel the intent of diminishment from the father and could see the son hanging on every unspoken word. I could also feel the instant heat shoot through my body, a heat distinct from the sun we were all sharing. The boy continued to look at his father, the father looked on, and I moved on. I felt sad for the boy and for the heart that produces such hateful programing. While I didn't take the incident personally, it did leave a sour taste in my mouth that the sweetness of my mango margarita couldn't mask.

Like it or not, the ways of our parents and ancestors are with us, even when we don't know them, don't like them, or don't remember them. Our sense of self and our family both require each other and complete each other. Even though we grow up and change, we are who we are because of our parents and ancestors. In fact, what we have come to know as our individual selves is more an experience of relativity or kinship with agency—the ability to make choices and be influenced or shaped by the choices of others. The bottom line is that, whether intentionally or unintentionally, we pass on a patterning to present and future generations.

Early Trauma and Race

As individuals, we have all had a range of experiences—many joys and sorrows that have shaped our lives. Each of us has experienced physical and mental hardship, and some of us have carried an indescribable weight from past wrongs. We all have the indelible markings of trauma, timeless wounding, and the dignity of survival. Early traumas shape how we relate to life and to race.

I grew up in South Central Los Angeles. In our family of eight, we raised each other. Our family and the working-class neighborhood where I grew up were preoccupied with surviving. My mother worked multiple jobs, including being the choir director for our church. We were hardworking and responsible. We paid our taxes, were faithful churchgoers, looked after each other, and were intensely active in the civil rights movement. In our neighborhood, people struggled with mental illness, domestic violence, addictions, and stress-related health challenges. There was financial and emotional distress in most families due to widespread unemployment, discriminatory hiring practices, police brutality, and gang violence. Growing up, I experienced significant trauma and despair that shaped my individual and racial identity.

For example, I can never quite shake the image of my great-grandmother, day in and day out, pacing the floor in ceaseless worry about her children and grandchildren. She was in her eighties, and she worried because, despite a life of social activism, she could not protect our black bodies from the hatred and harm that infested our community. I remember how helpless I felt not being able to comfort her. She died with a broken heart when I was just seven years old, and it was then that I decided, *I'm not going out this way. There's got to be a better way.*

A second potent trauma for me was when I gave birth to my son and said to my mom, "I feel excited, and I'm also scared, and I don't know why." To which she replied, "Because you've brought another black boy into the world." I will never forget the solemn look on her face. It was as if she were saying, *Better toughen up, girl!*

In my family, we were raised to distrust white people. My mom told us that white people were not trained to care for us. I was frightened by her response and felt a bit claustrophobic, because in every direction it appeared to me that black bodies were expendable. So, I toughened up. You could say I became an example of Tina Turner's song lyrics: "Who needs a heart when a heart can be broken?"

Two years after the birth of my son, my father, forty-nine and a successful business owner, was shot and killed by his girlfriend in a jealous rage. I was seventeen, and oddly, I don't remember feeling traumatized. What I remember most was how tightly I held on to my two-year-old son in the back seat of a black limousine as we drove across town to bury my father but were stopped every few blocks by the National Guard because of community lockdown due to the Watts Riots. This shock left me questioning the value of life and plunged me into years of righteous rage. One result was that, at the age of twenty-seven, I had open-heart surgery for a mitral valve prolapse. Strangely, the white surgeons, whom I was taught not to trust, had my life in their hands and, in fact, had more access to my heart than I did.

I'm from a lineage of warriors and worriers, raised in an atmosphere of racial anxiety and racial jeopardy plagued by fear. To this day, I feel deep sadness for my great-grandmother who worried herself to death, for my father who was killed at the prime of his life, for my son who couldn't understand my need to cling to him, and for my own heart, which needed more than I could give it at the time. These traumas are part of my racial inheritance. The senseless and incessant suffering of my great-grandmother, father, and many others like them that was passed on to me had to be understood, dignified, and transmuted. Their lives changed the trajectory of my life, sending me on a spiritual inquiry into how I was relating to life, and influenced my life's work and, to a large degree, the writing of this book.

Early traumas live in the neighborhood of present-day racial distress; it's where they find expression and seek release. When we find ourselves in racial distress, an early trauma often co-arises and then intensifies what is occurring in the present moment. For example, to this day, when a black body is killed by the police and repeatedly made visible in the media, they all look like my father to me until I blink a few times. This clearing of the eyes is important. It allows me to decouple—to distinguish the past from a full experience of the present, both horrible and distinct experiences.

What's Unfinished Is Reborn: Historical Racial Trauma

The term *historical trauma* was first developed in the 1980s by First Nations and Aboriginal peoples in Canada as a way of explaining the ongoing, intergenerational impact of despair experienced in their communities from genocide, loss of culture, the intentional spread of disease, and forcible removal from family and communities. Enslaved blacks in the United States also experience historical trauma. Much harm was inflicted on black bodies who were deemed chattel, including separation from families, branding, whipping, shackling, mutilation, and rape. When harm of such magnitude is deliberately inflicted, it makes the trauma more difficult to overcome psychologically, snowballing into communicable social disease that affects generational well-being for all of humanity.

As an example, we might look to the historical trauma of lynching in the United States. It is well documented that lynching blacks was often a festive family occasion for the white people performing the lynching. As I reviewed the history that occurred for generations in the South and examined the photographs of white boys and girls, who stood near their excited parents and watched the burned or hanging bodies, I wondered how those children were feeling. What was happening in their hearts and minds? They were not the direct perpetrators of these actions, but they witnessed a horror that was deemed normal. Were they frightened? Did they have questions? Were they opposed? What was required of them to fit into that moment? What would have happened if they had objected or resisted attending? What price did they pay emotionally and spiritually to maintain belonging? How did they have to behave to ensure love and acceptance? How did they adjust their hearts to reside with such human hatred? What did they do with their feelings? Surely they had some. Did it affect their ability to be intimate, alive, or empathic? What kind of adults did these white children become? What did they teach their children about race or the value of a life? What human price over the generations was paid for such denial, dissociation, rage, and amnesia? What unfinished business was passed down to the next generation?

We might also imagine what was in the minds and hearts of the black families as they helplessly witnessed such hateful acts from afar or who may have dreaded that such evil could occur when their son, daughter, father, or child didn't return home at the end of the day. What stopped them from going insane or erupting in a rampage? What behavior was required to survive? How did they adjust their hearts to exist with such human hatred? What did they do with their feelings? Surely they had some. Did it affect their ability to be intimate, alive, or empathic? What kind of adults did the children become? What did they teach their own children about race or the value of a life? What human price over the generations was paid for such suppression? What unfinished business was passed down to the next generation?

How might these historic crimes, which continued into the 1960s, live in the hearts and minds of individuals and groups today? For example, how do American Indians cope, generation after generation, with a history of deliberate exploitation and extinction as a social norm? How do black parents cope, generation after generation, with losing members of their family to murder and imprisonment as a social norm? And how do white descendants of such crimes reconnect to life by owning the soul death that accompanied such loss?

How do these generational traumas, and so many like them, impact the racial narrative we live in today? Might they have something to do with how we have become either desensitized or overly sensitive to racial harm? How might it help us understand the criminalization and mass incarceration of dark bodies in the United States and Australia? The increase in gun purchases by US citizens? The killing of unarmed black bodies by police nationwide? Or the bold eruption of white supremacy in the White House?

One need only think of what happened to Sandra Bland just a few years ago to recognize that these traumas are not just a thing of the past. In 2015, Bland, a twenty-eight-year-old black woman and civil rights activist, was arrested after being pulled over for not using a turn signal. She verbally resisted, clearly claiming her rights. The video of her arrest showed the white police officer becoming increasingly irritated by her outrage and her threats to report the officer's wrongdoings. Bland was forced out of her car; photographs after her arrest showed her bruised and what appeared to be drugged. She was later found hung to death in a temporary holding cell under police custody. We can't know what actually happened, there were no cameras; however, it's not farfetched to conclude that this was a modern-day lynching, condoned by institutional racism, by unexamined yet continuous generational racial hatred of white supremacy.

What's unfinished is reborn. Institutional racism and historical racial trauma have generational impact, causing substantial and long-term damage to our cultural and psychological well-being. It's important to understand this stained soil of US history and to recognize how white supremacy has systematically and intentionally resisted human equality in favor of power and greed and how this cultural swamp has impacted us all.

As individuals, no one is exempt from individual and generational trauma—the unnerving vulnerabilities that follow us around like a shadow. For many POC, this early wounding was pointedly about race. Racism was and continues to be the injury on top of more commonly shared social sorrows. Some white people I have worked with also share that they have experienced racial trauma, commonly sharing that they feel shocked and frightened by the rage or other emotions expressed by POC. When asked what they feel about race when such distress is not prompted by POC, many whites describe themselves as feeling uncomfortable, confused, numb, and vague. One white woman described it as haunting, and a white man said it felt like flu symptoms. These descriptors of fear describe a subtler form of racial trauma common among white people—racial trauma that has not been vetted.

POC may tend to be more aware of racial traumas and less aware of childhood traumas, whereas whites may be more aware of childhood traumas and lack awareness of race or racial traumas. Some of us can't bear either, while others of us hold on to old racial views and beliefs out of an unconscious loyalty to our parents and ancestors—our pledge of allegiance, so to speak.

When our racial inheritance is unknown or ignored, we contribute to racial ignorance and suffering and, through our actions, proliferate the unfinished business of our parents and ancestors in present and future generations. Racial ignorance and injury will continue until our history, hearts, and minds are transformed. What pains you to recall as you reflect on your racial identity and history? What racial traumas were passed down from your parents and ancestors, and how have you dealt with them?

It is important to acknowledge and attend to our racial programming and suffering. Shame, secrecy, and complicity will often distort and obscure the hurt and harm that are right before us. Such traumas, whether known, unknown, or invisible to others, give birth to racial biases, shaping our perceptions, thoughts, and emotions and influencing our actions. Old trauma, once a wound, is now a scar; yet when brushed against, we are reminded of what must never be forgotten—the suffering that broke our hearts and woke us up.

Racial Group Identity

We belong to many group identities that make our lives complex and rich; examples of these identities include religion, education, marital status, age, physical and mental abilities, talents, gender identity, sexual orientation, economic class, country of birth, and race. Regardless of our understanding or estrangement to race, as individuals, each of us holds membership in racial group identities—to name a few, American Indian, Alaska Native, Australian and Canadian aboriginal, Hispanic, Latino/Latina, black or African American, white, Asian, Native Hawaiian, other Pacific Islander, and multiracial people. These racial group identities extend our individual identities.

We all belong to a racial group identity or identities, whether we like it or not and whether we know it or not. It is important to both understand and manage identity dynamics from two perspectives: (1) our direct experiences as individuals within our own racial group identity and (2) the projections that other individuals and races place on us and our racial group identity.

One way to illustrate how we project onto group identities is with an exercise that I often offer in the Mindful of Race training. In the training, I divide a large diverse group into several small groups. Each group is given a flip chart and markers. I shout out a race or ethnic group—for example, blacks, whites, Jewish, Irish, Mexican, American Indian, or Asian. Within each small group, members are instructed to call out, without hesitation, everything they have ever heard about that group, while the scribe captures what is said on the flip chart. After about two minutes, they are asked to turn the chart paper over and are given a different racial group. This goes on for several racial group identity categories. The participants then have the opportunity to add additional race identities or ethnicities, all captured on chart paper.

I then instruct the groups to organize all the like racial categories from the several small groups and post them on the wall, so that several different reportings are clustered together. Participants are then instructed to silently walk around the room and read the posts. I then invite participants, who stay in silence, to stand next to the charted racial group that represents their most challenging racial group identity—whether their own or another. A few moments are allowed for everyone to notice in silence where people are standing and how this visual picture affects them. Finally, each person is invited to share with the large group how these charted impressions have affected not only them personally but also their families and communities.

In this exercise, we readily see how we have been shaped and influenced by others within and outside our racial group. What's on the wall is how the collective consciousness perceives group identities. We all have heard it, sensed it, and may even believe it. We can also see in this exercise the discrepancy in how we perceive a racial group (group identity) and how we feel about the people we may know who are standing next to the charted information (individual identity). When we project in these habitual ways, we perpetuate a collective view or belief that the individual or racial group has not consented to. Such projections are not necessarily untrue, but they are not absolutely true, nor are they the only truth. We see the dual challenge inherent among racial groups: (1) what we know to be true about our racial group identity and (2) the perceptions and projections we must manage from those outside of our group experience.

Racial groups, explicitly or implicitly, shape our views and influence our behavior. They govern the conduct required to maintain racial group membership. They also determine how we relate within our racial group and how we relate to those outside of our racial group.

Acknowledging our individual and racial group identities helps us see our complexity and diversity. We can then begin to recognize that we are all, at our core, good individuals, capable of learning and changing for the better. We all have independent biases and prejudices—a natural by-product of our being human. We have all experienced any number of joys and sorrows, and we are each searching for the same thing—to live freely and peacefully together, wherever we can, without harm and without a gripped heart. Our human challenge as racial beings is to ensure that all of us enjoy this safety and freedom.

Racial groups are structural ways of relating in relative reality, but they are not all treated equally. Some racial groups are dominant, while others are subordinated. As we will discover in the next chapters, dominant groups have the power to inflict their biases on others, while subordinated groups do not.

3

Racial Group Dominance and Subordination

n my diversity trainings, I commonly ask, "What is the profile of the dominant group in North America?" People reply immediately and cynically: white, male, Christian, heterosexual, married, able bodied, with upper-class conservative values. When asked, "What group identities are subordinated in North America?" I hear women, blacks, Hispanics, American Indians, elders, poor people, disabled people, the planet herself, and gays, to name a few. Dominant and subordinated group dynamics are deep in our psyche and are reflected in the world in which we live. This is our social conditioning cultivated over many generations—approved of by some, glossed over by others, and gravely impacting most.

We can begin to notice within ourselves, within our own group identities, and within society at large certain characteristics common among racially dominant and racially subordinated group identities.

Given the complexity of the human race, many of us hold membership in both dominant and subordinated group identities. However, most of us identify more immediately with our subordinated status.

White people, for example, commonly recognize and talk about their own subordinated group identities more readily than they do about their race or dominant group identity. A few examples from the Mindful of Race training program: A white gay male can speak of his subordinated status as gay but avoids

Characteristics of Racial Group
Dominance and Subordination

Dominant Racial Group WHITES	Subordinate Racial Group POC
Defines social norms	Reacts or assimilates to social norms
Controls resources	Fights for resources
Social presumption of superiority	Social presumption of inferiority
Eager to fix racial problems rather than to experience or understand roots of racial problems	Wants racial problem to be acknowledged, felt, and understood to ensure problems are uprooted
Does not notice or understand subordinated racial group experiences	Notices and understands dominant racial group experiences, as their lives depend on it
Individual identity focus; is unaware of being a racial group with infringing impact	Group identity focus; is aware of being a racial group that is infringed upon
Common mind-set: "Convince me why I should care."	Common mind-set: "You won't get away with harming us."

exploring his dominant group identities in race and gender. A white male (both dominant group identities) who transitions to female is shocked at how she is treated as a woman (subordinated group identity). A white woman is outraged that an Asian woman is not responding to her subordinated status of having chronic fatigue; rather, the Asian woman is relating to her as a privileged white woman (dominant group identity). In these examples, we see white individuals who are unaware of their dominant group identity as white (and its impact) and who are, instead, more aware of their subordinated group identity.

Conversely, subordinated racial groups must learn how to navigate white dominant culture, often while attempting to survive within it and change it. For example, an Asian woman tolerates sexual advances at work by her white male bosses so as not to rock the boat and to keep her job. A black father must teach his son how to behave when pulled over by the police, knowing that his son may do all the right things and still be killed. A half-black/half-white woman is seen as black in society and resents that there is no comfortable or welcoming way to express her full racial experience in either white or black groups. A Mexican undocumented worker is deported after working twenty-two years in the United States, forced to leave behind his American wife and two high-school children. A Jewish woman is internally conflicted, as she can choose to identify as subordinated in ethnicity and dominant in skin privilege and often chooses the latter.

We all want our pain to be recognized and acknowledged. Yet, the denial of or resistance by white individuals to white group identity causes much harm and separation within and among races. To understand the dynamics of racial dominance and subordination, we must look at group habits of harm, rather than solely looking at individual acts or single incidents.

Individuals can have preferences, biases, and prejudices, but they alone do not have the influence to dominate another race.

Dominance is about racial group prejudice plus power—the power to make racial group prejudices the norm. A white Canadian (dominant group identity), who is critical of the persistent talk of racial tension in the United States, shared, "We've moved beyond race in Canada. The US can learn from us." Yet she is dumbfounded when she is invited to examine the First Nations history and generational distress of the Metis, Inuit, and urban aboriginal peoples of Canadian land (subordinated group identities). When whites are unaware of or disown whiteness and white group dominance, ignorance becomes harmful.

What are you curious about as it relates to your racial group identities? What beliefs do you have about other racial groups that cause you inner distress? Acknowledging racial dominance and subordination helps us begin to see habits of harm. It also helps us own our roles in causing and relieving harm as individuals and as members of racial groups.

Racial Dominance and Racism

Those who cannot remember the past are condemned to repeat it.
GEORGE SANTAYANA, *Reason in Common Sense*

Racism is a tightly woven thread in our global social fabric. It lives in the minds and hearts of leaders and is reflected in the institutional policies, laws, and practices that govern the quality of our day-to-day lives. Racism occurs when dominant group culture, whether knowingly or unknowingly, both now and in the past imposes its values and beliefs on other races as the social norm and standard. Racism is difficult to comprehend when we look from the individual identity lens. To understand racism is to examine not only the systems, policies, and practices that ensure it but also the forces that resist changing it.

Since the origin of the United States, the institutions that govern this country have pursued white supremacy and have disadvantaged POC. Racial oppression—in particular, colonization, slavery, and slave mentality—has been and continues to be the bedrock of this country.

Every president since the beginning of US history has been challenged to address the moral and human injustices and civil rights of its people, especially black and dark bodies and poor people. Most whites in power have leaned toward advantaging themselves and those who look like them.

In the 2016 documentary *13th*, African American director Ava DuVernay brought attention to the Thirteenth Amendment of the US Constitution, passed in 1865 after the end of the Civil War. This amendment theoretically outlawed slavery, except if individuals were deemed criminal. This film turns attention to how the amendment has been used since that time to maintain slavery and justify racism and mass control, colonization, and incarceration throughout our nation's history.

Roger Wilkins, civil rights activist, professor, historian, and 1973 Pulitzer Prize winner, is quoted as saying, "Blacks have a 375-year history on this continent: 245 involving slavery, 100 involving legalized discrimination, and only 30 involving anything else." That "anything else," in my opinion, speaks to the present-day practices of racism without it being called racism. For example, anyone who watches the media can recognize the common portrayal of black Americans as criminals. Such repetitive public depiction, going back at least to the 1970s and especially since the age of all things videotaped, desensitizes the social mind in ways that deaden the human spirit. It then becomes "natural" or "right" for the average person to follow suit and then act hostilely and violently toward blacks and dark bodies. This "naturalness" includes how blacks see each other and the ensuing black-on-black violence. We are all susceptible to these racist portrayals, but many do not see this as racism. Rather, they are seen as "anything else"—as isolated criminal incidents.

A white woman who worked in a juvenile detention center proudly told me she spent many hours with black kids, helping them understand that they had committed a crime and helping them take responsibility for what they had done. This is fine, but only part of the solution. What she was unable to see was the majority of people in the detention system were black and brown. When viewing a social problem from the individual lens of unacknowledged dominance and privilege, what is often not seen are systemic policies, practices, and norms that result in a sea of dark people *detained* in the system. To understand racism, however, is to see the *systems* of oppression that maintain racial dominance and subordination.

Many want to believe that because we had an African American president, we no longer have racism in this country. However, looking closely at how the laws of governance worked against President Obama in his two-term presidency, both as a human and as a success, what a trained eye sees is racism on a grand platform. What has been true in the United States is that with any expression of racial progress (for example, having a black president), we experience the whiplash of racist resistance. Today, we see this whiplash in Donald Trump, who, has made it his priority to erase all things Obama, while also inciting expressions of white nationalism and extremism throughout the White House and across the nation through his policies, executive decisions, and laws.

Institutional racism—through policies, practices, and laws—are fed through the consciousness of its leaders. Leaders naturally influence work culture and define social norms. Because whites predominately head up institutions, corporations, organizations, and governance, creating them in their own image, the racial consciousness they bring to the culture often lacks an understanding of white group identity and its historic privileges and impact on other races.

To say an institution, corporation, or organization is racist is simply to say that its culture is oppressive, even as it may be unaware of the racial harm of its dominance. And how could it be any other way? How could it be anything other than whites in powerful positions, surrounded by other whites, feeling like good individuals without an awareness of whiteness or their racial group identity and its impact? Because the work of whiteness has not been examined, subordinated groups are left to push against a denied white dominant culture that has the mind-set: *Convince me why I should do something differently?*

When white individuals are not aware of their membership in a white racial group (for example, leadership), when they have not examined what it means to be white with other white people, they are able to maintain themselves as good individuals, therefore maintaining their dominant group status without being aware of or responsible for its collective impact on other races. This is how racism is perpetuated—the privilege of not knowing or caring.

There is no shortage of present-day examples of radicalized enforcement and extremism or of the brute privilege and impulse of white-skinned "saviors" perceiving dark-skinned people as "criminals" and having the individual power or the leadership representation to execute those beliefs. We need only look at our systems. For example, what goes hand-in-hand with the criminalization of black and brown people is the privatization of the prison-industrial complex that profits from them, or what Canadian author and social activist Naomi Klein refers to as *disaster capitalists*—institutions that profit off the disadvantaged.

Systems of racial oppression—in particular, slavery and the slave mentality—have been and continue to be the bedrock of this country. Michelle Alexander, African American, civil rights litigator, legal scholar, and author of *The New Jim Crow: Mass Incarceration in the Age of Colorblindness* (2010), described the War on Drugs as a deceptive strategy to militarize the police forces, terminally criminalize black people and black communities, and populate the growing privatized prison-industrial complex. The warehousing of black bodies and the laws that follow prisoners after release brand blacks for life, just as Jim Crow laws and acts of physical hatred branded former slaves. Current laws ensure that, once imprisoned for a felony, blacks lose their right to vote, to get jobs and housing, and to take care of themselves and their families. The formerly incarcerated are basically relegated to second-class status, not unlike life under Jim Crow laws, making them vulnerable to and targets of harassment, harm, and prison recidivism.

Racism lives in the institutions and systems that govern social well-being, profiting a minority of white people at the expense of the majority of people—largely, POC and poor people. According to Dr. Robin DiAngelo, white researcher and author of *White Fragility: Why It's So Hard for White People to Talk about Racism*:

> Whiteness scholars define racism as encompassing economic, political, social, and cultural structures, actions, and beliefs that systematize and perpetuate an unequal distribution of privileges, resources, and power between white people and people of color. This unequal distribution benefits whites and disadvantages people of color overall and as a group. Racism is not fluid in the US; it does not flow back and forth, one day benefiting whites and another

day (or even era) benefiting people of color. The direction of power between whites and people of color is historic, traditional, normalized, and deeply embedded in the fabric of US society.

Because racism is so intricately woven into our social fabric, it is difficult to both discern and discuss. Yet, fundamental to understanding our habits of harm is acknowledging and contemplating the stained soil of racism and racial trauma in US history. Racism is a human capital system driven by greed and fear—a fear of losing power and a fear of payback. Whites especially must acknowledge among themselves that they have a racial group identity. As a collective, they must also acknowledge how they have historically resisted racial equality in favor of white power and greed.

Aware of the insistence of subordination driven by dominant white culture, subordinated group members will, out of necessity, organize to represent their group identity in the oppositional stance ("You won't get away with harming us"), which has given birth to many civil rights and resistance movements over the centuries, including, of late, Black Lives Matter, Occupy, Women's March, Standing Rock, the Love Army Dream Corps, and more. These are acts of resistance to the oppressive and subordinated habits of harm perpetrated by white dominant culture. They are to be viewed as attempts to create a more balanced and just humanity.

4

Six Hindrances
to Racial Harmony

n this chapter, we look at six common and discernable hindrances to racial harmony. These hindrances illustrate the power dynamics of white racial dominance and POC subordination. They further help us see the relationship between individual and group racial identity. This list of six is not meant to be exhaustive, as there is nothing simple or clear-cut about racial dynamics; rather, the point of this discussion is to shed light on common habits of harm so we can interrupt our mental programming. We are not attempting to solve racial injustice or distress; rather, we are trying to understand their characteristics and see our relationship to it.

Some white readers may feel put upon by this discussion, and some POC may feel like they've heard this all before or that they are being painted as a victim. Keep in mind that the hindrances we're looking at speak more to racial group dynamics, not so much to individual actions. They are meant to stimulate deeper inquiry. When we think we know or we don't want to know, we stop being mindful, and by so doing, we live with a heart disease. Regardless of your race, I invite you to keep reading and to stay open.

HINDRANCE 1 White People, Good Individuals

As touched on earlier, a common disconnection between POC and whites is that the former tend to experience the world through group identity, whereas the latter tend to experience the world through individual identity. Many POC can readily relate to group identity because they live with the impact of race on a daily basis. They rely—and have relied heavily—on their group identity for refuge, support, and healing. Sharing like experiences—for example, by crying together, drawing strength from one another, strategizing together, and healing together—are ways in which many POC cope with the pain inherent in racial oppression and internalized oppression. Racial suffering has united POC, and most tend to believe that racial survival and progress have largely been due to the racial group and its many sacrifices. Thus, they may think, *Should I experience any success, I owe it to the group that supported me.*

Conversely, white people generally think of themselves as well-meaning, hardworking individuals, unaware of themselves as a racial group. Although many white people can relate to their families, religion, gender, or unique cultural experiences, rarely have they examined the collective, historic, pervasive, and often unconscious advantages of being a member of a racially dominant group. Of course, there are exceptions. Since the Trump administration, for example, we have seen an upsurge of white nationalism across the nation, advocating to maintain white supremacy. Such extremist behavior is what many white individuals fear they will be associated with if they claim racial group identity.

In a Mindful of Race training program following the 2016 election, several white men expressed concern that they were being treated as Trump supporters when they weren't. They didn't want what they felt was such a negative image to be projected onto them just because they were white. I waited a few moments before responding. Then I simply said, "Welcome to my world!" This is what it's like to experience group identity. People project and have both accurate perceptions and misperceptions.

However, individual members of dominant groups rarely taste their collective identity unless required to do so.

Outside of extremist behavior, when white individuals do consider their racial group identity and cultural conditioning, rarely is talking to other whites about race considered a priority for exploration or healing. As is characteristic of individual identity and dominant group identity, whites commonly assume that all they have done and become was the result of hardworking people who happen to look like them. Thus, they may think, *If I can do it, so can the next person.*

When whites of individual identity and POC of group identity enter into conversation—whites dominant, POC subordinated—great heartburn and division result. Most white people bring to the table their individual identities; they are unable to speak of their racial history or to own their dominant group status as a collective. Although POC can speak from their individual identity, their focus tends to represent a larger concern—the impact of racial harm on their subordinated racial group. Most POC are offended by white people's lapses in memory of their racial roots and their collective and continuing impact on subordinated racial groups.

HINDRANCE 2 **Internalized Oppression**

A sociological and psychological concept, internalized oppression describes when subordinated groups internalize the beliefs of the oppressor and, in turn, use these beliefs against themselves and other subordinated races.

Internalized oppression is an unconscious mental program that affects the psyche of POC. It is the cumulative consequence of being forced, over generations, to fit into a dominant culture in which every aspect of social life and racial meaning is systemically and structurally dominated by the white race.

Within this system of white supremacy, POC are intravenously programmed to fear whites and to fear each other; they are also programmed to aspire to whiteness, while also being forced to maintain racial subordination. The internalized effect of this programing is that POC aspire to dominance and, in so doing, subordinate other POC.

The programing of psychological oppression in the United States can be traced back at least to the sixteenth century. William Lynch, a British slave owner in the West Indies, was invited to the colony of Virginia in 1712 to teach slave owners his method of slave control. His infamous talk on the bank of the James River, entitled "The Making of a Slave," guaranteed that, if followed, his method would master the psyche of slaves into full submission and respectful allegiance for three hundred years. Lynch offered specific instructions, including the following:

> Use fear, distrust and envy for control purposes; distrust is stronger than trust and envy stronger than adulation, respect, or admiration. You must use the dark skin slaves vs. the light skin slaves, and the light skin slaves vs. the dark skin slaves. You must use the female vs. the male slave, and the male vs. the female slave. You must have white servants and overseers who distrust all blacks. It is necessary that your slaves trust and depend on you, love and respect and trust only you.

Lynch proclaimed that if these methods were used intensely for one year, the slaves themselves would remain perpetually distrustful of themselves and obedient to whites. While there is controversy over the authenticity of the Lynch speech, such strategies were consistent with the deep conditioning of white supremacy that governed those times.

This psychological strategy of white supremacy has permeated social life in the United States and those countries that aspire to be American. What gets internalized within subordinated racial groups is the belief that POC are unworthy, that they should be fearful of whites, and that they should distrust each other.

Internalized oppression stifles the very life force of the human spirit. It pits subordinated groups against each other, hinders racial healing and visioning, and limits the full bloom of a diverse humanity. The energy expended in questioning, doubting, and even fighting for white acceptance often takes POC away from knowing each other as a body of color and from caring for each other and themselves. It has them believing that to be as close to white power as possible is the mark of success. POC may feel temporarily favored or special—or to be "the only one"—all the while remaining unaware that they have modeled their ideals after the oppressor in hope of acceptance and achievement. Yet, they discover again and again that this aspiration is a false refuge. White dominant culture seems to never forget that POC are not white, even when POC forget.

HINDRANCE 3   **Stars and Constellations**

There are certain things we have been conditioned to see and not see as they relate to racial harm. One way I explain this is through a metaphor of the stars and constellations. For example, on a clear night, an innocent eye would see a multitude of stars on display in the sky, whereas a more educated or discerning eye might see various asterisms—groups of stars that form patterns or constellations like the Great Bear, Orion, or the Little Dipper. Such is also true with noticing the patterns of racial suffering and seeing racial habits of harm.

A group of concerned citizens attended a facilitated dialogue in Charlotte, North Carolina, to discuss the killing of eighteen-year-old Michael Brown, an unarmed African American man shot at least six times by twenty-eight-year-old white police officer Darren Wilson in Ferguson, Missouri, in 2014. This was one of many such public killings over a span of months, resulting in a nationwide outcry and broad shows of resistance. After watching a video of the killing, the group, mostly comprised of whites, were asked to share how they would describe what happened and how they felt about it. Paraphrasing, a white male in our group shared, "I can't believe that police officer killed that boy in cold blood. I'm outraged!" He was shaking and had tears in his eyes. He was describing a "star of harm"—an isolated incident.

When it was my turn, I shared, "I am tired of white police officers killing unarmed African Americans. I'm outraged!" I too was shaking and had tears in my eyes. I was describing color—a "constellation of harm"—a pattern. In his description, the white male saw this as an unfortunate incident—a single star; race was not a factor in view. For me, race was not only a factor, it was the Big Dipper—a repeating "racial group" pattern that I had been forced to acknowledge again and again.

This painful dynamic, when made obvious, is why some whites will say, "I'll just keep quiet and stay out of trouble because I don't know how to be politically correct." However, what is said is not as problematic as what it's rooted in, and silence is not the answer, nor is it refuge. A shift in how we perceive is required to transform habits of harm—to see not just the stars but also the constellations.

It's not just a handful of police killing black bodies that is the pattern. Although we could point fingers at the individual police officers, it is the system that fails us. A few of the unarmed African Americans killed by police within the past few years include Philando Castile, Terence Crutcher, Sandra Bland,

Eric Garner, Michael Brown, Rekia Boyd, Sean Bell, Tamir Rice, Freddie Gray, Danroy Henry Jr., Kendrec McDade, Aiyana Jones, Ramarley Graham, Amadou Diallo, Trayvon Martin, John Crawford III, Jonathan Ferrell, and Timothy Stansbury Jr. Common to all these killings is that none of the police officers was convicted. The constellation of harm here is embedded in the system that condones such behavior as normative, or what is referred to as *structural racism*.

When we begin to notice the constellations instead of just the stars, we can see the same patterns of harm toward aboriginal and native people, dark bodies, and immigrants throughout the United States, as well as in Palestine, Syria, Tibet, Australia, Bosnia, and Canada, to name a few. We can also see systemic patterns that are dependent on these oppressive dynamics, such as a growing militarized police force and a prison-industrial complex to house so-called criminals.

These struggles interconnect; they are not separate. The roots are maintained through dominance driven by greed, ill will, and ignorance. We all must think about things together that appear to be separate.

A white male prosecutor attending the Mindful of Race training shared with me, rather casually, that he had put many black men in prison, stating that he felt people should pay for their wrongdoings. He seemed to have no awareness of how such a comment would land on me—an African American great-grandmother who has many friends and family members inside the prison system. His belief is individualistic and only partially true. He described his job as looking at an incident, the facts before him, a case—a star. However, the prosecutor's role is not the only dynamic at play here. There is also the lack of awareness of being a white male, holding membership in an unexamined white group identity with power and history that systemically oppresses dark-skinned bodies. Granted, understanding whiteness is not a part of his job description, but it does not eliminate the fact that the constellation of dark bodies is systemically oppressed by structural racism.

What whites can do with the power they have to "prosecute" other races, officially or unofficially, is organize as white groups and ask deeper questions. They can question, for example, the ideology of "bad people" deserving to be punished. A more contextual inquiry might ask: "How is it that our legal system methodically incarcerates a predominance of POC? What beliefs, policies, practices, and politics sustain this system of racial oppression? How are we, as whites in power positions, profiting from punishment and benefiting from not challenging systemic inhumanities? What beliefs are we reinforcing?" These questions would challenge whites in power to see the constellations of harm and to examine who or what is on trial. They would also challenge individual whites to "member" themselves and become a racial group, instead of benefiting as passive individuals protected by job descriptions that sustain the machine of structural racism. It would be wholesome for all of humanity if white people, as a collective, were to see themselves as racial individuals and to recognize whiteness as a racial constellation with roots, history, power, and privilege that negatively impact other races, and then to organize themselves to dismantle racial constellations of harm.

HINDRANCE 4 **Intent and Impact**

Commonly, whites see the stars of intention and miss the constellation of impact, while POC are offended by the constellation of impact, which, in turn, can narrow their view of white intent.

Jerri, a forty-nine-year-old African American woman who attended the Mindful of Race training, asked, "How would you respond to a white woman friend of twenty years who says to you, 'You look like Aunt Jemima?'" Awfully hurt, offended, and speechless, Jerri had stopped all communication with her white friend after the friend had replied, "You're taking this entirely too personally. I thought our friendship was beyond race!" Jerri's face was quivering, and her hands were in constant movement as she shared the impact of this experience. Her visible agitation presented as trauma seeking understanding and a dignified release, not just catharsis. She cared about this friend of twenty years, yet she was too hurt and angry to engage and had since ignored her friend's endless attempts to communicate.

Jerri's experience is not uncommon and is an important one for examining the racial dynamic of intent and impact. The quandary for POC in this common hindrance to racial healing is that the choices never feel so good. While both the intent and the impact can result in hurt feelings for all, the burden of communicating the impact of intent weighs heavily on POC or the subordinated group. This means that, in addition to being triggered by the good intention of whites, POC must also find a way to communicate with whites—ideally without emotion or perceived threat—the impact of the white person's actions at a time when POC feel most vulnerable and activated.

Again, typically, white people enter engagements with POC as well-intended individuals, unaware of themselves as a racial group with historic baggage. Instead, they see themselves as a good guy, a white ally, an exception to whiteness, and they expect to be accepted as they are. POC, in an attempt to be with white people they like or must engage with, will often overlook white ignorance expressed in innocent intent. You could say that they collude with just being individuals and avoid discussing race. In fact, Jerri shared that she and her friend of twenty years had never talked about race.

In the absence of talking about race, there is an assumption, especially made by whites, that we are all good individuals, which is code for we are all the same—which means to whites, that "we are all like me." For some POC, there is an internal dialogue and tightening that they have learned to tolerate. Jerri chose to engage her white friend at the individual level and to avoid discussing her experiences as a racial being. Sometimes POC will make this choice out of pure fatigue; other times, to fit in or be accepted. When POC make this choice, however, they commonly tolerate, overlook, and accumulate any number of awkward or ill-expressed intentions made by whites.

There is another response to impact common among POC, and that is to confront white intention. With this choice, POC experience high distress and fear that their response could be written off as being overly emotional, cause discomfort or fear in whites, or result in loss of control in themselves. What's being fought against, often unknowingly, is the dread many POC feel in knowing that the oppressed are expected to guarantee the safety and comfort of the oppressor.

Commonly, white individuals have good intentions but are unaware of their impact on POC. As a result, when whites and POC engage, POC must risk confronting white intent either by sharing its impact or by choosing not to.

Whites commonly ask, "Why do POC separate themselves and form their own groups?" Let's look closer at this question. The question acknowledges white group identity—an "us"—while at the same time denying it. The question that could be asked by whites is, "What exactly are POC separating themselves from, and why?"

Jerri decided to send her white friend of twenty years an email, which she shares below:

Dear Old Friend,

I know that you would like to connect and explore what went wrong between us, but I'm still riveted by your comment: "You look like Aunt Jemima." I'm pretty hurt and confused, and I'm taking this time to care for myself. I don't have time to take care of your needs at this time. In fact, the thought of explaining my feelings to you only enrages me. I would suggest that you get with other white people who might be able to help you understand how such a comment would sever a relationship. You need to figure out how to wake up to your whiteness, and I need to take care of the wounding your comment created in me and further explore the assumptions I made of our relationship. Please stop calling me and respect the distance I need for now. I will let you know when and if I have a change of heart. I trust you will somehow understand. This is the best I can do right now.

Jerri

The hindrance of intent and impact is amplified at the institutional level. For example, white leaders commonly comply with the principles of diversity and inclusion by hiring or inviting POC into leadership or project roles. While this act has good intent, it often falls short of acknowledging differences and considering what would ensure an inclusive and welcoming culture. Without such consideration, POC are tokenized. The institution appears to be diverse, when it is actually only window-dressing diversity. White leaders and institutions commonly and unconsciously assume that POC who are invited into the institution should not only be grateful but should also want to be like the white people who invited them. The impact of such blind and commonplace assumptions for POC, who at some point recognize this dynamic, is that POC must take on a second job—that of pointing this out—or decline what appears to be an opportunity.

There are also those times when POC can point out impact not from a place of activation but from a place of clarity. After several days of teaching in Washington, DC, I was able to score tickets to the Smithsonian National Museum of African American History and Culture. My partner and I took a taxi to the museum. After clarifying our destination, the driver, a middle-aged white male and acknowledged Trump supporter, shared that he had never visited the museum and was disturbed because the building's design stood out like a "sore thumb" on the Museum Mall. He stated with puzzlement, "Why couldn't they make the building fit in with the other museums on the Mall? What does it have to look so different? I think it's the ugliest building I've ever seen. It simply does not fit in."

My partner and I, two elder black women sitting in the back seat of his car, looked at each other with clear eyes. I replied, "That is the story of our lives in this country as black Americans. We don't fit in and don't want to fit in. And why should we? The museum is about us defining ourselves and sharing our history. Of course it would look different from any other museum on the Mall." To which he replied, "Hmm, I never thought about it that way." To which I replied, "I hope you have a chance to visit the Museum. It will likely give you more to think about."

Here we have a white male (dominant group identity) assuming whiteness as the norm (why does this museum have to be different), yet unaware of his history, of his privilege, of whiteness as a social norm, or of his impact on two black women in the back seat of his car (subordinated group identities). Of course, he has a right to his individual opinion, but it lacks rootedness in whiteness—his racial group identity and its impact.

When such innocence occurs as frequently as catching a cab or being out with long-standing friends or coworkers, POC are challenged with both managing whatever distress the comment may trigger and with trying to determine whether to point it out. Seldom can they simply enjoy the ride.

Regardless of race, we must all concern ourselves with both intent and impact and do what we can to wake up and minimize harm of others and ourselves.

HINDRANCE 5   Cumulative Impact

Cumulative impact refers to the long-standing weariness and wounding that subordinated groups experience in their day-to-day lives. It's an experience of battle fatigue in that it speaks to the incessant need to confront racial indignity, harm, injustice, and danger. It's like a repetitive motion injury that occurs daily, weekly, and generationally, impacting the capacity of the body and the mind to function optimally.

Cumulated impact is not something POC set out to express. Rather, it piles up inside like trash; when jolted by white ignorance or injury, it crashes all over the place. This loss of control is fraught with anxiety and fear, as well as righteousness and embarrassment, and it distorts and further intensifies racial distress.

You could say that cumulative impact reflects a collective anxiety held by POC due to the imbalance of energy and care required by all to adjust to the weight of racial suffering. Cumulative impact is revealed in conversations across race and particularly in conversations about race, as illustrated in the earlier example with Jerri.

Think about it. From the beginning of this country to this day, POC have had to fight for the right to be treated equitably.

From the most blatant display of the prison-industrial complex to what is now referred to as micro-aggressions—those innocent comments and innuendos expressed by white people—it all adds up in the course of a day and a lifetime.

White people are unaware not only of the cumulative impact that POC carry from historic and present-day racial ignorance and injury but also of their role in contributing to it. Therefore, whites have not shared this concern or shared this weight. Understandably, we bring an imbalance of energy to our engagements with each other.

As white people move through the world as good individuals unaware of their racial impact as a group, POC are the recipients of such innocence and ignorance multiplied by hundreds, or even thousands, over time. For POC, the skin is sensitive and irritated from such constant exposure. With nerves on edge and vulnerability on high from the cultural conditioning of racial harm and generational injury, POC enter racial conversations fraught with tension and fear. Inwardly, they experience a kind of allergic reaction and outbreak from the repetitive injury of racial distress. This often results in a disproportionate distressed response, and both POC and whites may ask, "Where did that fury come from?" Of course, it's not always fury. POC may withdraw emotionally or physically to ensure a sense of safety and relief.

It's difficult for white people to hear about being white because they don't associate themselves with white group identity. Therefore, they tend to take the information personally, reacting with fear, guilt, and shame. Then they will do everything in their power to put out the fire—fix it, make it go away—to distance and not feel what is actually happening. In their reactivity to cumulative impact, they don't ask questions to deepen understanding, nor do they acknowledge how awkward they feel or how afraid they are. It simply looks like

POC have a problem. In such moments, POC are required to manage not only their own emotions but also the inadequate response from whites.

Cumulative impact has a profound effect on how we relate to each other—in particular, on our capacity to feel safe, stay present, and deal with the discomfort and perceived threats. We usually think our reactions to racial intensity are exclusively our own, but all of us are a part of a much larger tapestry of nerves and history. We all feel more than we understand or can remember.

Brain research can help us understand cumulative impact. The amygdala is located in the limbic region, an older part of the brain rooted in survival. Its function is to experience emotions, perceive threat and danger, and respond based on information from past experiences. When we feel threatened, the amygdala is triggered and hijacks the middle prefrontal cortex region of the brain. The middle prefrontal cortex is a larger, ever-evolving part of the brain that manages our capacity to reason, conceive actions, and respond to the present moment without layers of emotionality and distortion. It's the part of the brain that is uniquely human, empathic, and relational; it is where we negotiate fairness, mental well-being, and a felt sense of freedom. When this area of the brain is hijacked by emotions (the amygdala), our nervous system tilts off its axis, and we literally can feel as though our lives are at risk—and too often they are.

REACTIVITY REASONING

Cumulative impact is also reflected in the reactions of communities of color whose lives have been disenfranchised by structural racism—policies, laws, and attitudes that make caring for oneself or one's family challenging and racial inequality commonplace.

A white male in the Mindful of Race training asked a sincere question: "Why do African Americans run at the sight of police officers or give police officers such a hard time?" There was no simple answer to this question, nor was there an answer that would fit every situation. Both racial inheritance and cumulative impact are at play. This question fundamentally reflects individual curiosity that lacks an understanding of white supremacy and its impact.

One way to respond to this question is to consider our conditioning within a broader historic and racial context. For example, in addition to the present-day profits from warehousing black and brown bodies in the prison-industrial complex and the militarization of many police forces, African Americans have good reason to fear the police and to be outraged by the social perception that they are, by default, criminals. Being perceived as criminals, African Americans know that daily their lives are at risk. Of course, we all have the human instinct to survive. Some African Americans will contest the police, and some will run. Many have been killed whether they run or stand still, whether they are silent or openly hostile. Whatever the response, the amygdala is in high activation; everyone is overwhelmed. Such responses are rooted in cumulative impact.

Police officers are sanctioned by their membership in the dominant group—police. They are not separate from society; rather, they reinforce the consciousness of society, and, like society, they are conditioned to fear and perceive African Americans as criminals. Both African Americans and police officers perceive threat and respond from conditioning with the power they have available to them. For many African Americans, that power is their physical bodies. With police officers, that power is their weapons. Both views are conditioned in the mind from social and past experience, reinforced in the brain through repetition, and expressed via the nervous system through the body by actions using the power at hand.

Our racial conditioning and reactivity are intimately woven into our beliefs and intertwined with our nervous system. When our mental capacity to reason is hijacked by the amygdala into hysteria or righteousness, the brain's executive function is offline, and we react based on old fears and beliefs, instead of responding to the present moment.

Cumulative impact reflects a generational imbalance of racial care. Our instinct to survive is not the problem, but how we are conditioned to perceive threat is a problem. To uproot habits of racial harm requires soul searching at the individual, group, and institutional levels.

HINDRANCE 6 White Privilege

What has commonly been coined "white privilege" has to do with the group power or racial dominance that white individuals can blindly exercise. The nature of white privilege is that whites either don't recognize they have it or feel entitled to it. White privilege is having the choice to be white or not, to claim membership in a white group identity or not, to be aware of race or not, and to talk about race or not—all without consequence.

The term *white privilege* often turns off white individuals or makes them angry. While some white people can relate to being white, many have difficulty relating to the term *privilege* because it has not been their "individual" experience. Whites would say that their success is the result of hard work, and no doubt it is. However, privilege is the water that dominance swims in, and it is impossible to understand it when we look solely from the lens of an individual. To understand white privilege is to understand the characteristics of white group identity. This would involve white individuals claiming themselves as a race and engaging each other in their history, power, and impact on each other and other races. And this, by and large, has not been done.

Subordinated racial groups readily understand the term *white privilege,* as it frames a pattern, a constellation, a characteristic of white group identity disowned by whites, whose impact has a painful and pervasive bearing on their individual and group lives. Most POC do not have the privilege of walking away from the wreckage of racial harm perpetrated by dominant white culture that wreaks havoc not only on families and communities but also on their individual integrity.

Gayle, a Hispanic woman and the only person of color on the leadership team in a large nonprofit, challenged a decision her white peers felt strongly about. A white male replied to her, "I can sense your anger. What can I do to help?" Gayle replied, "You can stop assuming I'm angry and deal with the issue I'm raising."

Many whites assume that a person of color is angry when that person is actually being firm and clear. This assumption is often an expression of privilege—an unconscious strategy of deflecting their own anger and fear. What is often unacknowledged in whites is the deep-rooted outrage that is stimulated when a person of color has the audacity to challenge them in any way—to confront, push back, or say no. It threatens the unacknowledged presumption of white supremacy. I'm reminded of slavery and the slave mentality, which has not been thoroughly healed in this country—blacks were not to look directly into the faces of whites, let alone have an opinion or a sense of self other than what whites defined. Most whites confronted by POC do not understand the deep roots of their discomfort; only that, oddly, it should not be occurring. In such instances, instead of the privilege of deflecting, whites have the opportunity to turn more inward and deal directly and honestly with their own discomfort and examine its rootedness in white conditioning.

While the weight of pushing against white ignorance and ill will is largely carried by POC, much of this work belongs to white people. Systemic racial harm and injury is not a POC issue—it is a white privilege issue.

What happens when white individuals claim a privileged group identity? As mentioned in chapter 3, those in dominant group identities generally feel neither the need nor the priority to examine impact; therefore, those who take such a risk often back down when they begin to feel awkward and confused. This discomfort feels threatening because it calls whites to challenge what has long been denied—that they are a racial group with work to do. The white person doing the confronting fears the loss of privilege—favors, resources, and relationships—in what has normatively been a disowned and unacknowledged membership in white group identity. Whites have the privilege of choosing whether to challenge this status quo. Because of the unacknowledged benefits of not challenging the status quo, many whites choose silence, distance, and safety over the discomfort of change, intimacy, and more honesty. This is how privilege works.

There is another, more pernicious white privilege at play across the United States—white nationalists and subculture extremist groups. Since Donald Trump became president, inciting aggression through vile speech and hostile tweets, an increase in vociferous hate has once again come out of hiding. The Southern Poverty Law Center maintains an updated database of the growing number of white nationalist hate groups across the United States. Many of these extremist groups are recurring constellations of harm and have no problem claiming white privilege and supremacy as their birthright. Many white individuals associate claiming white group identity with such groups and do not want to be linked with the groups' public hatred and righteousness. However, such a stance is an abandonment of white racial group members, and it keeps whites from examining the diversity or the shadow side of white group identity and its roots in historical privilege and harm.

Why is white group identity important to acknowledge and investigate? The answer is simple—relatively speaking, it exists. To avoid this examination is white privilege. Most people growing in racial consciousness would consider it major progress for the human race if white people were to not only recognize themselves as a racial group, with a collective history of dominance and privilege, but also to become attentively curious and diligent about how, as a race, they have become dis-membered as a group body as a result of that privilege. This inquiry would be a wholesome and healing use of privilege that supports bridging separation within white communities and between whites and humanity at large.

White Collusion

Collusion at the individual level involves acts driven by our conscious or unconscious need to maintain or gain group power. Other words that describe collusion are *indirectness, insincerity, avoidance, dishonesty, withholding, going along with, aligning, conspiring*, and *hidden agenda*. We collude to gain favor or approval; to maintain privileges or membership; or to play it safe, fit in, or avoid being a target of attention.

Our individual behavior in groups is influenced by our perception of who has power and how we gain the favor of a power figure. Collusion takes clues from our intuition or felt sense, rather than from what's stated. For example, we've all been in groups where we know who has "real" power and who the "real" players are. We then position ourselves according to what we are trying to gain or maintain. Such posturing for power is what's meant when people say, "You have to learn how to play the game."

Collusion is the nuanced way in which white groups maintain norms of membership—who's in and who's out and what's appropriate and what's not. White norms in groups commonly determine the degree to which someone can play the game, challenge the game, or be tossed out of the game. Fundamentally, when whites collude, they are betting that their choice to behave a certain way will get them more of what they want and secure group membership

Acts of racial collusion represent those moments of awkward edginess when whites are privately determining the level of risk they will take in questioning collusion or going against white group norms. There are three common ways to avoid this edginess: through blindness ("we don't see race"), sameness ("we stay around people who look like us"), and silence ("we don't talk about race—especially not about being a race").

BLINDNESS

Common to all of us is the fact that we don't see the world as it is but how we have been conditioned to see it. The delusion we carry is that everyone sees—or should see—the world as we do. What we see and don't see has consequences. In general, white people do not see race unless they feel threatened or until someone else brings it to their attention. For example, I will often hear white people in diversity trainings say to me, "But when I look at you, I don't see race." As an African American woman, this well-meaning comment from the lens of the white individual renders my experience as a racial group member invisible, my history whitewashed, and my people at continued risk. It's an innocence I can't afford to have. When whites don't see race when they look at me, they see me as an individual, just as they see themselves. In doing so, they deny my racial identity and group history—a history that their racial group is a part of subordinating. Given that my racial group identity has been historically denied respectful visibility and equality, such a statement, and many like them, is more an insult than a compliment.

Racism—a group and institutional relative reality—negatively impacts POC with regularity. To not see race is the privilege of white individuals; it is a white group experience reflecting a disowned, denied, and unexamined group identity. It would be rare, for example, to hear a POC say to a white person, "When I look at you, I don't see race." This is because, as subordinated racial groups, POC must be attuned to race, especially whiteness.

In general, when race is brought to the attention of whites, the assumption is that race will be about "the other" and not about them. They may become confused and feel misunderstood; then they will go into defense mode, viewing any critique of their actions as an individual assault.

The 2016 US election was an example of white blindness. A few examples: Obscure language and false facts swarmed the media with such regularity that the terms *fake news* and *alternative facts* were considered truths by the administration. White representatives proclaimed a ban on people from certain predominantly Muslim countries entering the United States as a strategy to reduce terrorist threats. Although a ban on known terrorists from entering the United States might have been valid, it soon became a ban on Muslims. Another example is the view that the prison-industrial complex is not about POC; it's about criminals. Such blindness is oppressive; it is a blind eye to race that upholds white power.

SAMENESS

Sameness is both peculiar and common among whites. A 2015 Facebook post read, "Incoming Congress: 80 percent white male, 92 percent Christian, 100 percent unaware that this is a problem." Sameness is experienced differently depending on whether you are part of a dominant or subordinated racial group identity. There is comfort in likeness, in "perceived" sameness. Therefore, whether or not we realize it, we tend to naturally favor people who look like us and who reflect or mirror our beliefs and experiences.

POC typically threaten sameness not only through the color of their skin but also by daring to be themselves, which is predictably outside the confines of whiteness. For example, a white woman leader I coached shared how anxious and excluded she felt about POC regularly gathering at lunch, and yet it never occurred to her that her all-white leadership team had lunch together daily as well. Sameness as white privilege is like being fish in water, taking water for granted until we are out of it—taken out of our comfort and thrust into being more mindful of race.

SILENCE

Collective silence of white people is often used, knowingly or unknowingly, to maintain privileges in an unacknowledged but understood culture club. In such instances, silence is a way in which white privilege is exercised.

Whites will often be blind to the need to bring up race and will wait for someone else—whether another white person or a person of color—to speak of race. This usually defaults to POC, as their lives are more impacted by silence and they feel pressure to speak on behalf of racial group harm. When POC express their upset about racial actions and impact, whites become afraid and feel ashamed, guilty, or silently angry, regardless of how the POC communicated that upset. Some whites will cry; too often, tears become a way that white people silence POC and avoid being openly angry or clear. In turn, POC become even more upset, because their need has been distracted—they must deal with their own distress and the distress whites are presenting.

Silence in organizations speaks loud and is often a way for whites to maintain power and avoid being honest and direct, especially toward POC. Whites are often afraid of confronting POC for fear of getting it wrong or being accused of being racist. However, privilege can hide such fear through silence. For example, it is not uncommon for whites to create entire policies to avoid direct engagement with POC, to move POC to different jobs, or to offer a severance package instead of giving honest, constructive performance feedback that would likely deepen understanding and the relationship. Whites have also admitted to promoting POC to avoid working through a conflict with them. Fundamentally, when white people collude, they maintain privilege by avoiding the intense heat and creative chaos that is required to compost racial avoidance into racial awareness and honesty. When white people collude in silence, they are sheltered from racial literacy and intimacy.

Regardless of our racial group identity, silence can be dangerously complicit, and speaking can threaten our perceived sense of safety and acceptance among racial group members. Such discomfort calls us to deeper inquiry and honesty.

Part 1 Summary

Becoming aware of racially dominant and subordinated group dynamics is fundamental to transforming habits of racial harm. We won't recognize these dynamics if we look solely through the lens of the good individual; instead, habits of harm are readily discernable and important to discern through the lens of racial group identities.

Acknowledging racial group identity gives us pause. In this pause, we can begin to wake up to our racial habits of harm and ask, "In this situation, is my view reflecting my dominant or subordinated group identity? Do I believe this to be absolutely true? What is this conviction rooted in? What assumptions am I making about power or victimization? What can I learn or open to? What can I let go of? How do I act with clarity and in a nonharming way?" We can also begin to notice the racial group hindrances at play around us.

Our racial group identities are conditioned and complex. The point of painting this visible picture of our relative reality is to illustrate the need for a more balanced understanding of racial distress. We have all been trained to fear, fight, and ignore each other out of greed, avoidance, hatred, or indifference. We all have history and wounds, and we all have the capacity to transform.

The first part of this book has supported us in seeing our diversity and complexity and in acknowledging that we are individual racial beings; we hold membership in racial groups, and there are power dynamics that seed and feed racism, reinforced through institutional laws, practices, and policies that hinder social well-being and racial freedom. Understanding how we have been conditioned as racial beings to relate to others and ourselves is fundamental to transforming racism.

Racism Is a Heart Disease, *and* It's Curable!

Now that we have allowed ourselves to be diagnosed, we can move toward the surgical intervention of mindfulness and begin to unblock the arteries of racial humanity. The procedure will take some time, but the prognosis is promising.

Part 2

MINDFULNESS

~ HEART SURGERY ~

5

Life Is Not Personal, Permanent, or Perfect

Nothing we see or hear is perfect.
But right there in the imperfection is perfect reality.

SHUNRYŪ SUZUKI, Zen monk and teacher

As we begin to turn our attention inward, we often feel the soreness, tenderness, and vulnerability from the habitual ways we have met the rough edges of racial distress, and it is easy to feel overwhelmed. Although these feelings may be difficult to metabolize, it is possible to do so. Our thoughts and feelings are not permanent states; rather, they are crucial experiences to attend to, and it begins with understanding our minds. This is the role of mindfulness meditation.

Mindfulness has its roots in the 2,600-year-old tradition of Buddhism. The practice of mindfulness meditation supports us in experiencing more mental ease and harmony. It does not help us get rid of racial ignorance or ill will, nor will it erase anger or despair. Rather, it offers a way for us to slow down and investigate our experiences with care and wise attention. It supports us in bearing witness to our racial distress and conditioning without distortion, elaboration, or judgment. We can notice, for example, how racial perceptions live, what thoughts we are giving birth to, and how we feel thinking about them. We can acknowledge where we get stuck and discover what supports letting go.

Simply stated, mindfulness is the practice of present-moment awareness, with an understanding that what we are aware of has a nature, or what is known in Buddhism as the three characteristics of existence:

- The nature of impermanence: Change is constant, and all phenomena arise and pass away.

- The nature of selflessness: There is no enduring or reliable self; we are a series of ever-changing elemental processes, all arising and passing away. Who we are emerges out of interrelating causes and conditions.

- The nature of unreliability and dissatisfaction: "Shit happens," and we are not in control of having things go our way.

These natural laws, core to the nature of our existence, can offer insight into how we relate to racial distress—specifically, what supports more distress and what supports release from distress. Despite the painful truth that racial injury, ignorance, and injustice have spread virally throughout the world, the three characteristics of existence stand.

I have a simple mantra for remembering these three characteristics: "Life is not personal, permanent, or perfect." These natural laws are true to all existence. They are like gravity. Gravity has a nature—it's not personal. Once you understand gravity, you do not drop a glass and expect space to catch it. Seasons also have a nature—they are not perfect or permanent. Once you understand the seasons, you know how to dress and go out into the world. As the story goes, everybody is a genius, but if you judge a fish by its ability to climb a tree, it will live its whole life believing it is stupid. Fish have a nature. Fish exist in water. Fish do not climb trees.

Relatedly, race is not who we are. Race is a social construct that points out the nature of diversity. In and of itself, race is not personal, nor is it a problem. The problem is how we perceive race, socially project onto race, and relate to race as if it were personal (all about our individual or racial group experience), permanent (the idea that views about race never change), or perfect (the idea that whatever is happening should be to my liking or meet my standard of what's right). We are all perfect in our imperfection, which is always changing. In *Zen Mind, Beginner's Mind*, Shunryū Suzuki put it this way, "What we call 'I' is just a swinging door which moves when we inhale and when we exhale." When we don't recognize or comprehend the true nature of all existence, racial distress proliferates.

Over the years, reminding myself that life is not personal, permanent, or perfect has kept me from falling into sinkholes of despair and destroying rooms with rage. It invites me to pause and turn inward. It gives me a chance to ask myself, "What's happening? Where are you gripped right now? Are you taking this situation personally—to be a personal experience instead of a human experience? How many people before you have felt this way? Where else in the world are people feeling similarly gripped? Do you believe that how it is now is how it will always be? Are you distressed because you are insisting that this situation be other than it is, right here and now? How can you care for the pain you're in at this moment?"

Sometimes people, especially people who have been repeatedly and deeply harmed by racial ignorance and distress, think this approach sounds too passive, too compliant; they may feel they are giving up, masking, or glossing over injustice. But that's not it. To embrace our true nature is not to deny that racial injustice is not pandemic in society or that certain racial groups are not, in fact, targets of harm. It's about embracing the truth of what is actually happening in the moment with an understanding of its nature.

It is impossible to be unbiased when we are unaware of how we have been conditioned in racial likes and dislikes, fears, aversions, and judgments. In other words, racial distress is a real experience, and how we relate to racial distress is habit. Instead of being fearful of other races or convinced we know everything we need to know about race, an exploration of racial conditioning or habits of mind can be a gateway to deepening our understanding of humanity.

We are shaped by our conditioning, but we are also shaped by wise understanding and the quality of our awareness. When we are unaware of the nature and impact of our actions, we cause much unintentional harm. Entrenched beliefs and closed minds are what wars are made of. Our challenge is to become more aware. Mindfulness meditation is a practical way to transform our understanding and actions. It's not just a technique or mental exercise; it is a radical practice of self-compassion and respect that supports us in softening the rough edges of racial distress so we can untangle our habits of harm and respond to racial distress more wisely. I would go so far as to say that we need these practices to support us in staying present to the horrors of racial suffering and to experiencing freedom from it. Yes, I said freedom! Knowing from the inside out momentary freedom is a potent stabilizer when facing racial distress. Another way to say this is that through mindfulness practice we can know increasing moments of freedom within racism and despite it.

This law of all existence is difficult to grasp in the heat of racial distress. However, with mindfulness practice, we begin to recognize, through our direct experiences, that we can know a deeper freedom—a freedom that is not dependent on outside circumstances being different.

Addressing racism requires a multitude of individual and relational interventions. Sometimes we need to speak out and organize with others to resist systems of oppression. There are also times when we may need a good psychotherapist to examine our stories, unpack our traumas, and recognize the relational source of our wounding. Mindfulness meditation allows for yet another opportunity: wise awareness.

Without wise awareness, habitual patterns rule our lives. Our mind wraps itself around our views, our perspective narrows, and we tend to feel "dead right"—or just plain dead. With mindfulness practice, we learn how to get still and simply receive the present moment without preferences. We become interested in what's happening right now and the impact it is having on us. In this potent pause, we can ask, "Is how I am thinking and feeling contributing to suffering or to freedom?"

No amount of racial warfare or social resistance is more healing and sustaining than the freedom each of us is capable of experiencing internally, despite our circumstances, through mindfulness meditation. This practice brightens the mind, softens the heart, allowing us to see more clearly our own reflection and that of the world. With such clarity, we can do what must be done with care and understanding.

6

Establishing a Daily Meditation Practice

We are habitual beings. Some of our habits are intentional, and others are unconscious. The ways we have been conditioned to think about race and respond to race are all habits. The good thing about habits is that we can create new ones.

Everything we do with regularity is a habit. For me, meditation practice is in this category. It's a habit, a non-negotiable part of a daily hygiene routine—I shower, shave, brush my teeth, and meditate. In *Mindsight: The New Science of Personal Transformation*, Dan Siegel describes nine benefits to the brain and nervous system that can result through the practice of mindfulness meditation: regulating the body, attuning to others, balancing emotions, being flexible in our responses, soothing fear, creating empathy, cultivating more understanding, gaining awareness of our morals, and achieving heightened intuition.

Perhaps some of you already have a practice. For those of you who don't, I offer meditation practices here that will support you in being mindful of race.

Here are a few tips before we get started.

Find a Good Time and Place

To begin, identify a comfortable, quiet space where you can sit each day. Sitting at the same time each day has a positive, regulatory effect on your nervous system. If you are new to meditating, start with a short amount of time and gradually increase the time. I encourage beginners to apply the 5/5/5 Plan—meditate for five minutes a day, five days a week, for five weeks in a row. By the end of the five weeks, you will have a new habit. Sit long enough to feel yourself shifting toward ease. If you can't sit, simply occupy a seated position for ninety seconds.

Begin and end your meditations with intention. For example, I begin each meditation by lighting a candle while silently stating my intention. Through my example and my practice, may I be a light, radiating in all directions, for good. I then pay respect to my teachers and ancestors by calling out their names. After meditating, I offer a prayer of gratitude dedicating the benefit of my practice to all conscious beings throughout the world. I then blow out my candle. I may journal what I am feeling and thinking, and I may even outline my day.

Create a simple yet meaningful meditation ritual that frames your practice. Eventually, such a practice will be internalized and carried throughout your day. A consistent meditation practice deconstructs and reprograms the mind toward calm and stability and supports clarity and insight into our racial conditioning.

Pay Attention to Posture

You want to establish a posture that is relaxed yet upright. Consider the needs of your body and make necessary adjustments. Seek balance at six points:

- Your sit bones are firmly planted on your seat or cushion.

- Your spine is vertical without tension, as if the top of your head is being pulled up toward the sky.

- Your shoulders and hips are in alignment, and your hands rest open with palms up or down on your thighs. Feel this balance on the inside from the buttocks, up the spine, into the shoulders, down the arms, and into the hands.

- Your legs are crossed, if that is comfortable for you. If you are seated in a chair, place the bottom of your feet firmly on the floor with your knees about hip width apart. Use a pillow at your feet if they do not firmly touch the floor. Allow yourself to feel a sense of balance on the inside in the full volume of your legs and feet.

- Your eyes can be open with a downward diffused gaze a few feet in front of you, or they can be closed. Sense the balance of your eyes making contact.

- Your teeth are slightly ajar, which naturally relaxes the jaw, and your lips are lightly touching each other. Rest the tip of your tongue just behind your front top teeth. Feel the fullness of the mouth and a sense of balance within the mouth.

Establish these six points of awareness prior to any sitting meditation practice.

The meditation practices in the chapters that follow will support you in clearly seeing habits of harm and in relieving inner racial distress. We begin by cultivating calm through sitting and walking meditation, followed by a meditation practice of kindness that will establish an atmosphere that supports further exploration of racial distress and relief. I recommend that you practice them in the order presented.

Note: Meditations will be affected by what you eat and drink. Avoid meditating on a full stomach. Sugar, alcohol, and excessive carbohydrates have a sluggish effect on concentration and physical comfort. Become aware of how these substances affect you, and then make more skillful choices.

Let's begin!

7

Cultivating Calm

Sitting and Walking Practice

We must be still and still moving.
T. S. ELIOT, *The Four Quartets*

When a can of seltzer is shaken up, it is not the time to pop the top—unless you like to see eruptions. We must first set the can down and let the insides settle. The same is true for us. When we are shaken by racial ignorance and distress, we need to stop, get still, and allow the body and mind to settle, even to relax. How do we do that? How do we allow the body and mind to settle? It begins with body and breath awareness.

Sitting Meditation

Cultivating calm is fundamentally a practice of presence in which we focus on the breath and body and disregard everything else, at least for now. The mind's job is to be busy twenty-four/seven. Our thoughts and emotions are constant, often taking us away from the present moment. Thoughts and emotions are not a problem, nor will they cease to consume, overwhelm, and amaze us. In this practice, however, we are training the mind to focus on the body and breath.

To begin, establish your posture using the guidelines offered in chapter 6.

Body Scan

Start your practice with a body scan. Take your time as you move your awareness through the body, inviting awareness to relax each part of the body. Begin by bringing your awareness to the head and face, to the muscles in the face, to any tightness in the scalp—simply invite in a sense of softening. Next, move your awareness through to the neck and into the shoulders, bringing kind awareness down through both arms, upper arms, lower arms, the tops of the hands, all the way down to the fingertips. Bring your kind awareness to the palms of the hands and then the inside of the arms. Invite a sense of softening here, moving your awareness up the arms to the chest, the upper back, the abdomen, and then the lower back.

Bring kind attention to all the internal organs and muscles and the space inside the torso. You are just bringing a kind awareness to this area of the body and inviting a softening. Bring kind attention to the hip and pelvis region, the upper legs, the lower legs, the tops of the feet, the bottoms of the feet, all the way down to the toes. Next bring kind awareness to the insides of the legs and to the full length of the legs. Now bring your attention to the full body, softening through kind awareness.

Stillness of the Body

Sitting quietly, notice the experience of settling. Allow the mind to rest in the fullness of the body. Imagine the entire body as the mind. Feel the quietness inside the body. Rest your awareness here for the next few breaths. Begin to notice the stillness inside the body—it has its own experience. Open your awareness to noticing the experience of stillness. Settle the body until you begin to feel a shift in inner stillness and ease. Take your time to relax in the stillness of the body, firmly planted in your seat. Rest in the stillness. Notice the body steadying itself. Feel directly the body's movement, its graduation, and its gradation toward stillness. The stillness may not be dramatic, but you may notice a softening inside the body that you can rest in. Begin to feel the steadiness and stability that this stillness makes possible. Notice the quietness of stillness. There may be chatter in the mind, but it may be more faded and in the background of your experience, while the stillness is in the forefront. Give your full attention to the body resting in stillness, in calm abiding.

Let this experience of calm be fully known from inside the body. You may feel like a solid mountain or tree or like you have slid your full body inside a warm glove. Allow yourself to be with whatever the experience is for you. A natural awareness is made available to you simply through stillness, through calm abiding in the body.

Movement of the Breath

Next, begin to open your awareness to the movement of the breath—not to the thought of breath, but to the movement, the sensations of breath, that point of contact where the breath touches and moves the body. There is an experience of breathing that you can know directly. The breath is the body's most intimate and constant companion. Notice where the inhale stretches or expands the body and where the exhale collapses the body. Experience the sensations of the movement of the breath inside the body. Taking your time, allow yourself to know the stillness of the body and the movement of the breath.

Place your awareness on the exhale, riding the sensation of the exhale; feel the settling and ease that is the nature of letting go. Next, begin to experience the fullness of the inhale, then the exhale, and then the pauses at both ends. There is no need to manipulate the breath—just notice what it's like to breathe, the experience of breathing. For example, where do you experience the rise and fall of the breath in the body? In the abdomen? The chest? The tip of the nostrils? Give your full attention to this thing we call breathing. What is the quality of the breath? Is it fast, like a soft breeze, or is it a choppy wind? Is it faint? Are you holding the breath? Is it warm or cool? Is the inhale different from the exhale? Is it short or long? Be curious about how the breath is moving through the stillness of the body. Notice that the body is still, while the breath is moving. Both experiences are happening together—you are still while still moving.

Thoughts, emotions, and other sensations will arise in the body and mind as you practice. There is no particular reason for it, nor is it a problem. Keeping the body as relaxed as possible, rest in the full experience of the stillness in the body and the movement of the breath. Let both the body and the breath be known; let them be your primary focus.

Now, give attention to any experiences of calm in the body and mind. Slowly scanning the body, notice where you experience calm. Take the next few moments to notice how your body is experiencing calm and ease, however small. Know this experience as equanimity. Bring full awareness to the inner experience of calm. Allow the experience of calm to permeate and bathe each cell in your body, all the internal organs, and all the space within the body. Take as much time as you need to rest in the stillness of the body and the movement of the breath.

Some Closing Thoughts on Sitting Meditation

Sitting meditation is a beautiful centering practice that puts us in touch with our true nature; it shows us how nothing is personal, permanent, or perfect. For example, the moment we close our eyes, we readily see how busy our mind is—the constant change or impermanence of mind. We don't make ourselves think; thinking just happens. Thinking is impersonal. Although we may add to thoughts that arise, the arising of thought just happens—it's not in our control. In sitting meditation, we get in touch with our fears, discomfort, and distress—the hindrances of mind and the imperfection of moment-to-moment experience. Despite our mental activity, it can relax in the background of mind while we give our attention to the body and breath.

I encourage you to continue this practice daily. Start with five minutes. If you can sit for a half hour, that's even better. Sit until you can sense the experience of settling.

There will be times when you may need to do something active or more strenuous before your sitting practices. That's fine. Do that, and then sit.

In the early stages of sitting practice, you may experience a range of thoughts and emotions that shifts your focus away from presence. For example, you may experience the mind desiring to fix racial injury or plan a strategy to address social injustice. There may be thoughts or feelings of revenge or ill will, doubt, worry, restlessness, sluggishness, or boredom. Don't be alarmed by your thoughts or feelings, and don't give up. In this beginning practice, redirect your attention to the body and breath; more ease and inner stability will develop over time and that will support deeper understanding and inform wise action. Make sure you are seated comfortably in a chair or on a cushion. You can also stand while doing this practice.

Throughout the day, you might also want to reflect on the times of the day when you are most likely to be calm. Are there times when you are more calm than not? Notice how much importance you give to calm. Notice whether you feel guilty when you have a moment of calm, especially as you look around at the things in your life that must be done. Know that it is okay to have a reclaiming of ease in your life.

You might also begin to notice how you interrupt the natural moments of calm that are present, or you might notice when you are experiencing calm if there is a tendency to fill your awareness with something else. Most of us have an addiction to intensity and an adverse reaction to ease. Be aware, without judgment, of your tendencies.

When struggling with my own thoughts, engaging others, or in the thick of a racial conflict, I try to keep at least 50 percent of my awareness on the body and breath. I often ask myself silently, *How is the body feeling? Where is the breath? Can I be more at ease in this moment?*

What supports you to be calm? See if you can cultivate more of that. What are some of the more common conditions that cause you to lose calmness? Are you aware of when calmness shifts? Which habits of mind generally flip you out of a state of calm? How does calmness affect your relationship to racial distress or your impact on others? How does it inform what you do next?

Sitting meditation practice supports us in knowing, from the inside out, that we can rest in the body and use the breath as a calming inner resource, despite external circumstances. This is an essential practice for establishing the awareness and stability we need to investigate our habits of harm.

Walking Meditation

Core to being mindful of race is our ability to "stand" the truth of what is right before us and to walk aware of our intent and impact. Doing so requires that we live as fully as we can within the body in the present moment. Walking meditation is a mindfulness practice that supports such awareness, balance, and ease.

Walking meditation is helpful when you feel agitated or when you find yourself knotted in thinking. This practice shifts you from your head, through your body, down to your feet—to the ground of the matter. It supports relaxation and mental and physical balance and stability. The practice is simple because it is the practice of going nowhere, yet it brings you directly into presence and supports you in staying present. You are not trying to achieve anything or fix anything. The practice is simply about grounded awareness—an awareness that reduces obsessive thinking and other distractions—and is an excellent way to be present throughout the day.

There are many ways to practice walking meditation. The practice I offer here is what I have found helpful from my own experience on long meditation retreats. When practiced regularly, it strengthens our ability to be centered despite our circumstances.

GUIDED MEDITATION   WALKING PRACTICE

Allow a minimum of fifteen minutes for your walking practice. Find a quiet place where you can walk back and forth for anywhere from fifteen to twenty-five steps in each direction.

Begin by standing, bringing full awareness to the bottom of the feet equally balanced as they make contact with the floor or ground. Keep the body upright and relaxed. The chest and head are raised. The upper body should not be leaning ahead of the feet. Don't allow the chest to collapse or the spine to curl. The gaze is downward and not tightly focused. You can place the right hand over the left wrist or clasp the hands behind the back. Establish these connections with ease, releasing tension throughout the body.

Begin to slowly walk at a pace that maintains awareness and balance. With each step, feel the heel of the foot firmly touching the floor or earth, followed by the ball of the foot, including the large and small toes. Put equal weight on all four points as the foot touches the floor. Feel the foot firmly planted on the floor and notice how this foot balances the body, making it possible for the other foot to rise, swing, and plant itself on the floor. Again, feel the foot firmly planted and balanced on the floor. Feel the sensations on the bottom of your feet and lower legs. Maintain a pace that keeps you most present. After you have taken fifteen to twenty-five steps, stop and be aware of the transition from one direction to the next; the pause, the pivot, the turn, and the standing with two feet together, hips' width apart, before one foot is lifted for that first step. Repeat your walking meditation for a minimum of fifteen minutes.

Some Closing Thoughts on Walking Meditation

Consider walking meditation physical rehab for the heart and mind. In this practice, we are discovering, step by step, the experience of walking—something we do a lot but are not aware of. This practice, regularly repeated in the course of a fifteen-minute walking period, sends a message to the mind that we can carry our own weight and balance our own lives. This is not a thought; this is a potent, direct experience of stability, quietude, and ease.

Just as there is much movement on the earth, the earth itself offers us a sense of stillness. Such is true with our bodies. With momentum and consistency in this practice, we can begin to experience the stillness of the earth joining with the stillness in the body, and we can feel that there is no separation. This connection supports us as we move through our day-to-day lives—we can tap into stillness, regardless of the chaos that swirls around us. The steady pacing programs the brain to trust that we can rest in presence and move through the world centered and awake.

With consistency, this practice reprograms the nervous system to be at ease; we take our space and stand our ground. It brings stability and dignity to our form and to our hearts. We can imagine ourselves planting seeds of kindness into the earth with each step and pausing long enough in presence to add the warmth those seeds need to sprout.

Walking meditation is a simple, powerful healing medicine that develops mindfulness in our moment-to-moment lives. Just as we took our first steps as a child and discovered we could exercise more freedom, such is true over time with walking meditation. We discover, in walking, a wise and balanced effort from the inside out.

8

Kindness Practice

Love takes off the masks that we fear we cannot live
without and we know we cannot live within.
JAMES BALDWIN, *The Fire Next Time*

Be still. Gaze upon all things kindly.
GIL FRONSDAL

Kindness is the water of humanity. Without water, we harden. Kindness is an attitude, an aspiration, and a practice. It is also core to spiritual life and religions. In the tradition I'm trained in, we practice *metta*, which is the Pali word for unconditional kindness—friendliness and genuine acceptance. Metta is part of a constellation of heart practices referred to as the *Brahmaviharas*, or divine abodes.

Metta is not a prayer for help from something or someone outside of ourselves. It is not an ego-driven kindness based on possessions, attachment, or grasping, nor is it overly sentimental. Rather, metta is a genuine desire for all beings, without exception, to be safe from inner and outer harm, to be healthy and content, and to live with ease.

We all have ways of protecting ourselves from racial harm. We may strike out, walk out, or numb out, depending on the situation. Yet underneath all of our actions, despite appearances, is a shared and deep desire for kindness—to both offer it and receive it. We all wish to be able to stand in the center of racial ignorance and distress without parking our hearts at the door.

Metta is the antidote to such distress. It is the natural expression of the free mind; a state of mind that the heart naturally dwells in when we are not burdened by mental distress or distractions. It is often described as a feeling of well-being not dependent on external conditions, a quiet stream that is flowing at all times—a stream we can open to or know intimately through mindfulness practice.

The practice of metta supports us in priming the mind to embrace racial fear and distress in an atmosphere of nonresistance. The practice supports us in minimizing escalation and distortion by gathering the mind, focusing the mind, and steadying the mind in the present moment. It supports us in regulating our mental climate by adjusting the thermostat to care. When we do this, we are inviting the heart to open to warmth and genuine acceptance.

A metta practice will not make what we don't like go away, nor will it make what we do like stay. Through this mindfulness practice, we are not trying to change what we are facing. Rather, we are freeing ourselves in the moment by loving ourselves, and we are training ourselves to embrace what is right here, right now, with friendliness and intentional goodwill. But most important, it is about maintaining goodwill toward all, even toward our antagonists. Metta practice can serve as a radical blood transfusion, purifying generational patterns of racial ignorance, innocence, and hatred and opening the heart.

Years ago, I noticed the impulse to smile whenever I passed white people. I wasn't aware of intentionally smiling. Instead, smiling insisted itself into expression, an inward push outward that faintly felt as though my life depended upon it. Some of this action was due to the message I had received growing up not to be a threat to white people, which was no doubt a reverberation from my African ancestors. Somewhere deep in my psyche, I believed that if I didn't smile at white people, they would look at me with disdain or dismiss my smile and instead see me as the angry black woman that even I was convinced I was hiding.

As I practiced metta, I was able to view this impulse to smile in a different way. I could see how my mind fabricated fear by adding an old belief on top of the discomfort I was experiencing in the mere presence of white people. As I sat with that discomfort, I began to feel the weight and shape of this distress. It was as if I were wearing a tightly sewn mask on my face and neck.

As I offered kind attention to the distress itself, without the story I had about it, I began to experience fleeting moments of relief, even freedom, in between and beneath the distress I was experiencing. I began to feel lighter, brighter, more inner spaciousness, and my breathing was deeper and more even. It was interesting to notice that experiences of relief, as well as fear, came and went with shameless and unceasing regularity. In noticing both without preferences or resistance, I was honoring the true nature of their existence—not personal, permanent, or perfect. I could recognize how little control I had over their comings and goings and, while not always pleasant, how impersonal and impermanent the stimulation was—like a fly buzzing too close to my ear or the startle of loud music when feeling tender. This experience put a natural smile on the inside of my mouth.

It was in such moments that I began to have a true kinship with the subtle nature of metta and to discern that the deeper impulse to smile at white people—and all people—was older than my cover story. It was more like the innate gift of a singing bird or smiling baby. It was my true nature—that flowing stream we open to when we are open to it.

The impact of metta practice allowed more ease in my relationships with white people. As my body relaxed and my heart opened, I became less self-conscious of what white people thought of me. This release left me to experience what was actually going on, and I began to notice that smiling was a natural impulse of unconditional care—metta. Not only did smiling simply feel good, I also realized how much I needed to smile at myself. I delighted in the welcoming influence smiling had on others when offered and received without pretense.

A white dharma sister shared an eye-opening story of being at a political rally for Palestinian women in Northern California. She asked a Palestinian woman, "What can I do?" To which the Palestinian woman responded, "We like it when people smile at us."

Whether we smile inward or outward, the mind and heart respond well to kindness. The power of friendliness has an immediate impact on our body, our mind, and our nervous system. Research tells us that the feel-good neurotransmitters of endorphins, serotonin, and dopamine are all released when we smile. Friendliness and kindness are natural inner resources that can support experiences of freedom from racial distress.

Everyone has a cover story—a way we have been shaped to protect ourselves from the harsh realities of racial distress. Yet the simple act of smiling—this grace—keeps us humble and accepting of humanity and the vulnerability we all walk with. Those of us devoted to defrosting our racial conditioning can begin by cultivating an inner atmosphere of kindness through metta practice, opening the heart to bear witness to the intense energies of racial distress without turning away and without cover.

Metta is about kindness without exception, an indiscriminate friendliness—like the high noon sun that shines and touches all things. That's the capacity that metta represents. When we are in the practice of metta, we can radiate from the inside in all directions a friendliness that supports the well-being of humanity. The Dalai Lama said, "My true religion is kindness." That's a simple way of saying that kindness has everything to do with everything.

I would say kindness is also a decision—a decision to incline the heart toward goodwill for all beings, especially those who are suffering in racial ignorance, whether knowingly or unknowingly. It's a beautiful and natural way to extend the heart. It's something each of us can do, and I think it's something we must do. You will notice over time in this practice that the hard edges of a habituated gripped mind start to soften and the solid sense of self begins to dissolve, opening you to more warmth and space to rest and dwell.

GUIDED MEDITATION   KINDNESS PRACTICE

Begin by closing the eyes and relaxing the body using the body scan practices discussed in the description of sitting mediations (see chapter 7). Relaxation allows the body to soften into natural awareness.

Now, recall a moment of loving presence with another person or a moment of deep gratitude. Bring that recollection into your heart and mind. Allow yourself to recall that moment as fully as you can, as a way of igniting your direct experience with care, with kindness.

Imagine this person sitting before you right now, taking joy in you and wishing you well. If it helps, place both hands on your heart. Feel the happiness and the joy being exchanged between the two of you—that soft opening and acceptance, that allowing and relaxing that naturally happens when you are in the presence of a dear one or a precious moment. Don't let this just be a thought; let the body experience the thought, that memory.

Let yourself be touched by this recollection in this very moment, taking time to allow every cell in your body to be bathed in this loving presence. Rest here in the warmth of this recollection for a while—this is the experience of metta.

Now, with gratitude, allow the image of the person to fade away, but maintain the essence of loving presence, that powerful quality of kindness and care.

Offering Kindness to Yourself

As you sit in this essence of genuine care, use your entire body as you repeat the following phrases silently to yourself, allowing each word to touch you with care.

- May I be safe from inner and outer harm.

- May I be happy and content.

- May I be healthy and strong.

- May I live with ease and well-being.

- May whatever blocks my heart be dissolved.

- May I know joy and freedom.

- May I have food, shelter, and good care.

- May I be free from animosity and hatred.

- May I know peace.

- May I be a good friend to myself.

It helps to say the phrases slowly and to experience not only the words but also the spaces in between the words. Feel the good intention of these phrases as you say them in your heart and mind. Notice how these phrases are impacting your present-moment experience.

Feel free to experiment. If a phrase naturally comes to mind, offer it to yourself. Take as much time as you need to offer kindness to yourself. Notice how it feels in the body to make this sincere wish. Continue this offering using phrases that work for you until you rest with ease in an inner atmosphere of care.

Offering Kindness to a Challenging Person

Once you feel full or feel a sense of calm and stability from offering metta to yourself, you may want to offer metta to a challenging person. Bring to mind someone with whom you experience tension, difficulties, or dissatisfaction—perhaps a racial conflict toward an individual or leader. The challenging person may well be yourself. Allow the person to come clearly into your mind and heart.

Set an intention to keep your heart balanced and not to fall into reactivity, anger, or despair. If it helps, think of the other person as if they were at some distance from you. You might also imagine the other person as a child or newborn lying on a bed—eyes closed, breathing, small, innocent, and vulnerable. Notice how you feel as you invoke this image of the challenging person.

Stay with this image for a few moments as that person rests and breathes. If you want, you can come closer, sit by the bed, hold their hand, or just sit nearby. Just be there with them in this space of kindness, of tenderness. When you feel ready, offer the metta phrases:

- May you be safe from inner and outer harm.

- May you be healthy and strong.

- May you be happy and content.

- May you live with ease and well-being.

- May whatever blocks your heart be dissolved.

- May you know joy and freedom.

- May you have food, shelter, and good care.

- May you be free from animosity and hatred.

- May you know peace.

- May you be a good friend to yourself.

Notice how it feels in the body to make this sincere wish. Continue this offering using phrases that work for you. Take a few moments in silence to feel the kindness of your genuine intent to offer metta to a challenging person.

If it feels appropriate, you may wish to ask this person for forgiveness for some way you may have hurt them in your thoughts, actions, or speech, knowingly or unknowingly. Take your time and, with all of your imagination and genuine kindness, ask for forgiveness. You could also thank the challenging person for something you genuinely appreciate about them. Again, take your time to offer this sincerely and to feel this offer within.

Finally, allow the image of this person to dissolve. Return to noticing your body sitting here. Feel the state of your heart and mind—the quietness, agitation, openness, tightness, the reactivity, kindness, or whatever is there. Just stay with the stillness of the body and the movement of the breath. Notice if the challenging person is still challenging or if things have shifted within you even slightly. Take your time. Don't be in a hurry. Continue to rest in the body as you sit, breathe, and open.

Extending Kindness to All Beings

Just as you wish these things for yourself, remember that all beings, without exception, also wish to have this same kindness and well-being. Consider your family, a racial group, tribe, community, or the entire human race. Take some time to imagine the extent of their racial suffering and notice how you are touched by it. Reflect on your sincere wish that they be free from racial suffering and that all beings, without exception, be free from racial suffering. Then offer these phrases:

- May all beings be safe from inner and outer harm.

- May all beings be healthy and strong.

- May all beings be happy and content.

- May all beings live with ease and well-being.

- May all beings live with an open heart.

- May all beings know joy and freedom.

- May all beings have food, shelter, and good care.

- May all beings be free from animosity and hatred.

- May all beings know peace.

- May all beings be good friends to each other.

Extend this goodwill outward and indiscriminately. Notice how it feels in the body to make this sincere wish. Continue this offering using phrases that work for you. When the phrases naturally subside, rest in the radiance of metta, noticing the quality of your mind and heart.

Closing Thoughts on Metta: Kindness Meditation Practice

The practice of kindness, or metta, is simple but not always easy. It's simple because they are humble phrases that we offer to ourselves and then extend to others. The practice is not easy because we don't always feel loving or kind. When we are not feeling loving or kind, kindness practice is precisely what we need.

There are a few things to bring to mind. The actual phrases are not important; rather, they are pointers to well-being. What's important is the good intention and sincere wish that are motivating your genuine desire to offer the phrases. When you're not feeling it, return to the recollection of a moment of kindness you experienced from a dear one. As you bring someone or something to mind, you may not want to focus on your history with the person or situation. Instead, focus on a single moment when you felt your mind open and your heart soften. This moment may have lasted a split second or longer. The aim is not to attain some lasting or extreme state of mind but rather to remember that, despite yourself or your circumstances, you have been miraculously touched, even tenderized, by someone in your life. When you bring this recollection to the present moment, you are experiencing metta—the knowing of kindness. In this recall, allow your entire body to be full of kindness, taking the time to bathe every cell in your body in its warmth.

You may choose to modify the phrases so they resonate with your good intention. It is important that your phrases invite softening, acceptance, and kindness toward what's present, not phrases that crave for solutions or that tighten the body and mind.

The practice of metta is like composting. It may not seem like much is occurring, but deep inside the heap of your practice, good things are happening. In time, you will have rich, nourishing soil to feed and seed kindness. You could also consider metta practice a heart technology—a software upgrade you put into the hardwiring of your conditioning. The learning curve improves with consistent practice, with the cumulative impact resulting in an inner radiance that naturally opens you to noticing the good in others and yourself.

Metta practice is the antidote to racial ill will and aversion. It uplifts the heart and deepens the capacity to bear witness to racial distress without war. This practice supports quiet warmth and relaxation that extends to suffuse the entire body and beyond. It beautifies what is experienced, and it influences how we relate to what happens next.

9

Understanding the Cycle
of Misperception

Change the story and you change perception;
change perception and you change the world.
JEAN HOUSTON

Falling might very well be flying,
without the tyranny of coordinates.
BAYO AKOMOLAFE

The racial ignorance and distress we see in the world today is a reflection of the mind playing itself out in grand scale on the big screen, projecting our collective conscious and unconscious conditioning.

Every one of our lives represents a mosaic, with many shades, shadows, and shapes of experiences. In our relational world of vast diversity, kinship, and division, we have all been racially conditioned, trained through many generations in how to perceive race—our own and that of others. For example, when we look at people, we often reduce them to a concept or a summation of their group identity by saying or thinking superficially: "He's a gay guy" or "She's an Asian woman" or "They are black or white." So much is driven by the perceptions we have and by how these perceptions then feed certain thoughts, emotions, and beliefs. However, we were not meant to be simple summations or to be seen with casual eyes. We must be willing to look closer to see what else is there—to see beyond the glossy print of fixed perceptions to the nuances, the subtle gradation, the treasure in the understated, even the forbidden. This discernment begins within our own minds and hearts. We can become more mindful of our perceptions and use them as invitations to look more deeply at our racial habits of mind.

Buddhist teachings refer to misperceptions as perceptual knots—ways of viewing that block freedom and keep us entangled in knotty thoughts. These misperceptions include our attachments, aversions, distortions, and delusions. They keep us thinking that life is personal and permanent and that it should be perfect. One teaching in particular, the Vipallasa Sutta, speaks to the reinforcing mechanism of misperceiving—ways we distort reality to the detriment of belonging. Simply stated, we perceive something through our senses. There is a sense organ and a sense object—eyes see, ears hear, nose smells, body feels, tongue tastes, and mind thinks. Once we perceive, the mind habitually jumps to thoughts and feelings about what is being perceived; these thoughts and feelings are rooted in past experiences, past conditioning. Thoughts and feelings then influence the mood of our mind. When perceptions, thoughts, and feelings are repeated or imprinted through experiences, they solidify into view or belief. View then reinforces perception. This cycle becomes the way in which we experience and respond to the world.

We have racially conditioned perceptions that operate based on past experiences stored in the mind. These include memories, views, beliefs, and fears, all of which stimulate the mind to act or behave in ways that make sense to us. Once we perceive race, the mind immediately scans the memory bank of past experiences to interpret what is being perceived. We then add layers of meaning, and the experience shifts from bare perceiving into something more textured and nuanced. We refer to this in Buddhism as *papancha*—the proliferation or elaboration of thoughts and feelings. A few images might be helpful to understand papancha.

One image is cotton candy. It starts with a long paper cone that then weaves around a bunch of pink sugary sticky stuff spinning at high speed. It goes around and around and gets larger and larger, like matted hair. It is then handed to you to eat and enjoy. But it's messy at best and more fun to watch being made than to eat. Or you might think of a naked mannequin, which we then dress with layers and layers of clothing—or thoughts and emotions. While we all have our clothing preferences for comfort or style, we all start with a naked body or a long paper cotton-candy cone. Everything else is extra.

That's papancha, or the extra layers added to perception—interpretations, judgments, feelings, fears, and preferences. All are our own mental creations. When layered, perceptions become distorted, sticky, and weighty.

Essentially, we think we know something, and then we are off and running—all based on past experiences, preferences, and beliefs. And usually, but not always, it's all in our minds or, at a minimum, worthy of questioning. When we perceive and when thoughts and emotions are simultaneously activated, those thoughts and emotions proliferate, creating a state of fear and anxiety driven by what the mind is believing in that moment. In such moments, we are removed from presence; we vacate the premises of body and mind and are fixated on view. And the experience is real—until it's not. We're streaming the past live.

We feel more reassured when our views are mirrored back to us, even if we don't like our views. We are on guard when our views are challenged. Views that don't align with our own go unnoticed. We stop being mindful when we think we know, and that's when much harm can happen.

Years ago, my mom—who taught through stories and music—told me a noteworthy joke: On a one-lane zigzagging mountain road, two black guys driving down the hill pass two white police officers driving up the hill. They shout out to the cops, "Pigs, pigs!" The police officers, pissed by the perceived attack, keep driving. Seconds later, the police officer who is driving must slam on his brakes to avoid a herd of pigs crossing the road. This is the cycle of misperception at play.

Perception determines the characteristics of what it perceives—for example, whether a race is threatening or whether a race is worth paying attention to. It determines whether we like someone or something and whether we shoot someone or run. What we see in race is not inherently good or bad, right or wrong. It is our judgment about race—how we have been conditioned to think and perceive—that is problematic. We place judgment on what we perceive; we add layers of meaning—papancha.

There is much we can do. We can make a practice of questioning our perceptions and critiquing any views and beliefs that surface in our mind that work against clear seeing, belonging, and healing. We can choose to reevaluate our racial perceptions, thoughts, emotions, and beliefs; try to recognize where they come from; and strip them of all those extra layers. Until we are willing to examine our views of racial conditioning, we're flipping off a caution and could kill some pigs or end up dressing a mannequin in a penguin costume.

Understanding the cycle of misperception supports us in distinguishing habits of harm. How perception, thoughts, and emotions reinforce views is an important mechanism to recognize and a useful way to begin questioning our perceptions and critiquing views and beliefs that work against racial literacy, harmony, and freedom.

What we attempt to do in the mindfulness practice (described in the next chapter) is recognize the cycle of misperception and use our perceptions as invitations to look deeper to unknot inner distress and racial habits of harm so that our response to outer racial suffering can be attended to more wisely.

10

Working with Racial Distress

RAIN Practice

When we can sit in the face of insanity or dislike
and be free from the need to make it different, then we are free.

NELSON MANDELA

One of the practices commonly used in meditation communities for dealing with difficult emotions is called RAIN. It was developed about twenty years ago by longtime Vipassana meditation teacher Michele McDonald. It is an acronym for Recognize, Allow, Investigate, and Nonidentification. More recent developments refer to the "N" as Nurture, which is how I will use it here.

Although there are many variations of its use, RAIN is essentially a mindfulness practice that invites us to turn inward to work more intimately and more wisely with emotional distress. This practice is fundamental for investigating habits of mind that arise in the face of racial ignorance and distress.

Up to this point in the book, we have been working on establishing inner stability by cultivating calm through the body and breath in sitting and walking meditation, which are crucial foundations for our next inquiry—RAIN. RAIN practice will support us in understanding our relationship to racial distress.

In RAIN practice, we are not problem-solving an external racial problem or concern. Rather, we are examining our relationship to racial distress and learning how to bear witness to its nature—discovering directly that racial distress is not personal, permanent, or perfect. We investigate mental habits so that we can see clearly, as clear seeing supports wise action. Through this inquiry, we can understand and tame our habitual impulse to fight what is happening, avoid what is happening, or distort what is happening.

Awareness plays a critical role in investigation. Awareness allows us to see without overidentifying with what is seen. For example, awareness of anger is not angry. Awareness of fear is not frightened. Awareness is just aware—it mirrors back what is present without distortion. Just as the mirror reflects the whole body, not just the face or the hair, so our awareness should include everything, not just the aspects of ourselves we like. The mirror does not have preferences or an opinion about what appears, and neither does awareness. This is the true nature of awareness. When investigating our habits of mind, it can be helpful to open our awareness to include all that is in the mirror, without fixation or preferences.

With RAIN, we are investigating the unfinished business of the heart through the body. We are transforming our conditioning by seeing behind, beneath, and beyond the object of racial distress in service to freedom.

RAIN is most effective when done in sitting practice, after establishing a mind steady enough to support self-reflection. In this chapter, I discuss each letter of the acronym, followed by practice instructions for each. At first, try to complete each phase of this practice in one sitting. Once you feel you understand each phase, you may choose to use them as four separate practices. Initially, this practice cultivates wise agency over reactivity. Over time, it permeates our moment-to-moment lives.

R
RECOGNIZE: What's Happening?

Begin by stopping and taking a seat, turning your attention inward toward the distress, and recognizing what's happening. One variation on this question is to ask what's obvious in this moment.

The point is not to solicit the details of the distress. For example, you are not asking what's wrong, why this happened, or who's wrong. Instead, you are asking, "What's happening right now? What's obvious in my inner experience in this moment?" You are shifting from being ensnarled in the distress to being aware of it, from *identifying with* what is happening to *recognizing* what is happening. The inquiry "What's happening?" invites the mind and body to respond.

Simply notice and silently name what is happening. As you look at the activity of heart, body, and mind, what do you see and feel? You may mentally note, "I'm angry. I'm scared. I'm right, etc." Drop the "I'm" (not personal) and just use a word: *Scared. Angry. Right. Humiliated. Confused.* Notice and name body sensations: *Heat. Tightness. Pulsing. Shaking. Holding.*

When you ask, "What's happening? What's obvious in this moment?" you begin to recognize the thoughts and emotions that are taking birth in the moment. You can track what is happening as it is happening by noticing and naming what is happening. This subtle shift also supports you in discerning and depersonalizing experience. You simply characterize the experience by noticing what is happening and naming what is happening.

This inquiry short-circuits mental proliferation—papancha—and brings you distinctly into connection with your direct experience.

Noticing and naming what is happing shifts your attention. It is like aikido, when you step out of the direct charge and let it pass through. In this subtle shift, you take the standpoint of an observer of your experience, and the experience can feel less charged and less personal. By observing, you gain more agency and establish the foundation of mindfulness that supports clarity and presence.

A
ALLOW: Can I Be with What's Happening?

Once you recognize what is happening, ask, "Can I allow it to be known?" To allow what is happening is a crucial pause. When you allow, you are allowing the unfolding moment to be what it is without interference; without judgments, interpretations, preferences, or resistance; without trying to make it other than it naturally is in this moment.

Allowing is not the same as condoning experience. Rather, allowing welcomes and receives what is here. It allows you to soften around what is out of your control in this moment. This pause gives space to the energetic play of the distress; it is an exercise in showing compassion toward yourself. Mental phrases that support allowing include the following:

• This is hard. Let me be with it.

• Yes, this too!

• Of course, this hurts. Let me be with it.

- Yes, I'm afraid. Let me allow this fear.

- No wonder I'm angry.

- Confusion is like this.

- This is how it is right now!

- Let's be here together, dear one!

- I'm having a hard time, and I care about it.

To allow is to relax your sense of urgency. Such phrases soften the landing of racial distress, so you are able to rest more in awareness.

In the softening that results, you may notice habitual tendencies and impulses, the gravitational pull of likes and dislikes. You may feel pleasantness, unpleasantness, or numbness; notice how it is constantly changing. In not taking action—that is, not resisting what is—you may become acquainted with the wanting that drives your impulses and then allow this as well. You will experience relief in the body and mind when you allow what's happening, both the fullness of what you are experiencing and its release. Allowing reveals the true nature of not permanent and not personal. In time, you can begin to trust these waves of intense experience—and even relax into it.

I coach people of different races who are furious from encounters with racial ignorance and aggression. They can describe what happened in lavish and heartbreaking detail. They are often looking for confirmation, someone to see what they saw, feel what they felt, and even blame who they blame. Sometimes they feel foolish or defeated, beating themselves up for not responding or for not responding perfectly. But what they seek most is the experience of relief from the tension they are experiencing in the moment. They often think this relief is dependent on external affirmations, but this release comes not primarily from external confirmations but from inwardly yielding to what is actually happening. In coaching, I offer a place where people can express their distress and release it. I tenderly remind them that what happened to them perhaps shouldn't have happened, but it did, and what they have to work with in this moment is the impact the experience is having in real time. I invite them to turn inward to what's there and allow it.

This is not always a simple request. In such moments, many of us have been swept up by a trauma vortex or a flood of fear, and we might feel baffled, vulnerable, and at risk. We may be convinced that we know what's wrong and who's wrong. Something old, something borrowed, and something bruised is often activated. The more we resist fully allowing agitating thoughts and feelings to arise, the more we suffer.

Once when I was teaching a long retreat with a white teacher to a group of predominantly white practitioners, an Asian male new to meditation, who had been trying to ask a question for two nights, finally asked, "How do I stop my mind from being so busy?" My white co-teacher responded quickly and flippantly, "Stop feeding the monkeys!" The group broke out into loud laughter, but the Asian male broke into quiet tears. He was visibly shaken. He had taken a risk to speak, and the response he received from the teacher and group confused him. He didn't get the joke; instead, he felt humiliated. After I made a group intervention that pointed to the racial risk and injury and how we had all participated in it, the Asian male was able to experience visible relief. The innocent assault had been recognized and allowed, and the group, which was holding the assault as well, was also able to experience relief.

When I met with him shortly after, he voiced appreciation for the issue being pointed out and shared that he was most upset with himself for being so publicly vulnerable. He felt he should have been able to stop his tears. We sat with that for a minute or so. He shared that he had a long history of doing everything he could to perfect his environment so that he would be free from shame and criticism. I asked him how that was working for him, and we both had a good laugh. I then offered to him that it's okay to be messy, to be upset, even angry, about what happened. In the pause that followed, not only did he allow himself his forbidden feelings of anger through facial contortions and mild body trembling, but he also allowed himself to experience the release from the grip of perfection. I asked him to reflect on why he practices meditation. His response: "For moments like this."

Allowing cultural shame, anger, and vulnerability to be felt in his body, mind, and heart was remarkably freeing for him. Exploring his inner experience was more central to his freedom than engaging what happened in the meditation hall.

To allow is not to condone what is happening or what has happened; rather, it is to accept what is happening in this very moment. We allow what's here because it is what's here. It's like fine-tuning a radio station to rid the static of resistance or fear so that clarity pierces through. When we allow what's here, our energy is freed. It's not about fixing a problem. Allowing supports us in touching and letting go of the resistance to what's here—the good, the bad, and the ugly. It supports intimacy with presence.

To allow is to soften. Yet there are times when racial distress can feel too overwhelming or threatening for us to let our guard down. If we were to stay present to what is overwhelming, it might feel too intense. We would then lose mindfulness, become distracted, or stop caring. When we feel flooded like this, we can trust our instincts and not put ourselves in overload when our nervous system is advising caution. In such instances, a different kind of allowing is called for—backing off! For example, if something feels too intense, you can focus your attention on a comfortable or safe place in the body and rest there for several breaths, or you can practice one of the sitting meditations discussed earlier. If focusing inward is not helpful, you can open your eyes while sitting or do a walking meditation in which you take in sights, sounds, and smells. Or a good physical workout can support settling and release. If the intensity persists, you might reach out for help in a support group or to other professionals.

We befriend racial distress by allowing present moment awareness to permeate the territory of tightness. We pay attention without interference, without judgment, and without wishing things were other than they are. We allow the disturbance to be intimately known; we give it our kind attention. We reduce mental effort and urgency, keeping the body as relaxed as possible and the heart open.

To allow is to grow our capacity for both discomfort and ease, breath by breath. It supports us in surrendering to presence and is therefore a foundational phase in welcoming and respecting the experiences we are having.

GUIDED PRACTICE FOR **A: ALLOW**
Inquiry: Can I be with what's happening?
Practice: Yes, welcome. Yes, it's like this right now! Of course, this is hard! Yes, this too!

I
INVESTIGATE: How Am I Relating to What's Happening?

Often, the first two steps—recognize and allow—are sufficient for greeting, accepting, and releasing racial distress.

Other times, we need to go further—to investigate the ways in which we have become so knotted and explore how to further relieve the pressure.

Imagine that all distress has inherent wisdom and, when persistent, that it is calling us to a more intimate investigation. In asking, "How am I relating to what's happening?" we are not looking for a conceptual answer. We are turning inward and becoming more curious about the distress we are experiencing—its rhythms, patterns, beliefs, and places of aliveness in the body, heart, and mind.

Investigation is best done when there is some degree of stability in body and mind. When the distress can be allowed, it should be tolerable enough for self-reflection. If this is not the case, then we should first back off and practice one of the earlier phases of RAIN or practice the sitting or walking practices offered earlier until we feel stable enough to investigate. To investigate, we drop below the turmoil of our stories into the texture of bodily experience and discern how our perceptions, thoughts, emotions, and beliefs both fuel the experience of suffering and support its release.

Our experiences—and our awareness of them—are constantly changing. To investigate is not to assume that experiences will stand still until we conclude our study. Rather, to investigate is to experience impermanence with kind awareness.

Kindness and curiosity are equally important as we tenderly become aware of what we carry as racial beings, how we protect ourselves, why we hold on, and how we let go. Judging our experience is often an act of violence and self-hatred. When we investigate, however, we are practicing discernment, not judging ourselves. Discernment allows us to identify those mind states we want to support and those we want to let go. Nonjudgmental awareness, kindness, and curiosity are qualities that support investigation of racial distress and shift us toward release.

To investigate, the third phase of RAIN, you ask, "How am I relating to what's happening?" Begin by opening your heart and mind to the energy inside the body and how it is responding to what you have allowed. Become curious about your views, the deeper roots of your perceptions, and how they live in the body.

To investigate how you are relating to what is recognized and allowed, ask any number of questions, such as those that follow. Then pause and invite the body to be center stage as you look at how perceptions are being experienced and who you are without them.

- What's happening? What am I perceiving?

- How am I relating to what's happening?

- What racial views or beliefs are fueling suffering in this moment?

- What impact is my experience having on my heart, body, and mind?

- How does my belief impact my mood? Where is this felt in the body?

- What assumptions am I making? Do they support distress or freedom?

- Am I holding to an identity or view of dominance or subordination? Where is this felt in the body?

- Does this distress have an element of craving, selfishness, or ill will in it?

- Do I believe this experience to be personal or permanent? How is this belief experienced in the body?

- In my convictions, what's left out of view?

- As I track my changing experience, can I notice both the intensity and the moments of release?

- How is what's happening changing?

Often when we are tracking our changing experiences, images emerge. For example, one person described her inner experience of anger as a large wad of aluminum foil filling her head. Another person described his face as blowing a fuse. One person experienced release as a soft glove gliding across her cheek. Another described his chest softening as if sinking into a warm bath. Noticing the images, shapes, and colors of experience keeps us observing experience instead of merging with experience, and it makes investigation even more interesting. The key is to stay in the body of experience, not just in the head—not in concepts, papancha, or proliferation.

During a coaching session, Jimmy, a white male in his late sixties, heatedly and honestly shared:

I feel so uncomfortable in the diversity meeting at work. Every time a POC speaks, especially an African American, I feel certain they are going to tell me how screwed up I am and how my people are all bad—blah, blah, blah. I just want them to stop talking or to at least appreciate what I have done that is good. After all, there has been a lot I have done for them in the past. How quickly they forget.

I invited Jimmy to sit with his anxiety and track or investigate his inner experience with care and patience. I then asked him to journal what he was experiencing and discovering in his meditation practice. Following is his journal entry that he shared a when we next met:

> When I returned to my meditation practice that evening, I asked, "What's happening?" And I kept asking. Old memories began to flood my mind and rush through my body. I remembered that we had black nannies when I was growing up, and they were always so kind to me, even though my parents often treated them heartlessly and unfairly, and at times I too was unkind. As I allowed this memory to be known, I began to feel cold on the inside and clammy on the outside in my face and hands. It felt like a large, hard door had opened inside my chest—a door I wanted to close because of the draft of shame, but I couldn't close it. I allowed this intensity, and then my body began to settle a bit.
>
> Another thought arose: I realized that my irritation toward black people in the diversity meeting was connected to a conditioned expectation that black people should be more respectful and kind toward me without question. So when blacks showed anger and resistance in the diversity meeting, I was pissed. I felt the heat of anger pulsating throughout my body, and after a few minutes, it subsided, and I felt more open. As my body settled, another thought arose.
>
> I realized that underneath my righteousness was a faint need to feel loved by African Americans. I wanted them to forgive me for the secret I had not even acknowledged to myself until now. As I sit with

this sobering realization, I could feel what felt like inflation collapse inside my body around the heart. I then took the "me" out of the equation and began to feel the raw desperation of wanting—wanting to connect—something I had not done and didn't know how to do, not just with black people, but also with myself. In sitting with the rawness of wanting without fighting it or trying to cover it up, I realized that I needed to love myself, and I needed to nurture the desperation I felt with care.

I realized that this aching reached an intense peak and then died away. I could know its impermanence, and I could know relief from the inside and not be so dependent on black people changing to please me. This helped me be more at ease and able to listen and learn in the diversity meeting the following week. It took some time, but then I began to rest in a sureness that I could survive the discomfort and learn from it.

This type of insightful reflection is a gift to those of us who find it challenging to track and describe the movements of mind in the midst of distress. A discerning eye recognizes through this reflection that to investigate is not to solve a problem as much as it is to open to what is revealed, and then shift our relationship away from struggle toward freedom.

Often when we investigate, we notice what I call "frequent flyers"—those experiences that show up with regularity when we get still. Try not to be alarmed or surprised. Instead, expect them to show up. Create a place and welcome or allow them each time they appear. Be curious about what they want and need each time, how they are experienced in the body, how they change, when they come, and when they leave. They are visitors, not residents of the mind and heart.

To investigate, we bring awareness to what hinders and what heals. This includes an awareness of the spaces between occasions of distress—spaces of ease where we can learn to rest. By investigating, we strengthen our capacity to witness racial distress in our body and mind while cultivating a wise heart.

N
NURTURE: How Do I Care for This Distress?

The fourth part of the RAIN sequence is nurture—in this case, to attend to racial disturbance and let go. To nurture in this instance means to ask, "How do I care for this distress? What's needed? What facilitates release from distress?"

The kind of freedom we're talking about here is more than a wish and a prayer. It's an experience of softening and opening in body, heart, and mind. It's not about expending effort, as if we can force something to happen. It is about creating the conditions for release through wise mindfulness—recognizing and accepting, from our direct experience, that the nature of experience is not personal, permanent, or perfect. This understanding is what frees us even in the midst of horrible circumstances. We vacillate in our capacity to nurture distress. A lot depends on how attached we are to our view, identity, or an outcome.

Because the mind is conditioned to be attached mentally and emotionally, you must first ask the heart what's needed: "In this moment, what supports release? Do external conditions need to be perfect in order for me to feel relief? What's at risk if I let go, soften, and open? What supports freedom?" Ask, relax, open, and listen. In this important pause, you may realize that you need what I refer to as self-cooing. For example, you may need to say to yourself: "I'm here. We're safe. I forgive you. I love you." Or you can bring in other metta phrases like the ones described in chapter 8. Or you may nurture yourself by surrendering to a larger field of kindness with imagery—for example, the stability of a mountain, the vastness of the sky, the coolness of a still pond, or the warmth of fire. You can invite these images to care for and support you as you soften and let go (for more on this, see chapters 12 and 18).

Nurturing in this way requires that you suspend identification—that is, the view that what is happening is about you. Remember, it's not personal. As you open and soften your attachments and care tenderly for the suffering that the body, mind, and heart are experiencing, what happens internally? How does it feel to let go of your habitual thoughts? What are you left with in the absence of owning racial distress, of dressing the mannequin?

While at the airport, at the end of a difficult team-building session during which I had been criticized for pointing out something that was difficult to hear, I was feeling angry, jaw locked, and incompetent. My mantra of "nothing in life is personal, permanent, or perfect" was not resonating in the moment. I closed my eyes and took a few slow breaths. As I settled, an image of an old friend whom I truly loved (recognize) and the memories of times we shared filled my body with joy (allow). I rested in that recollection for a few moments (allow/nurture). When I opened my eyes, my mood had shifted, and I could reflect on the day (investigate) through a kinder lens (nurture). Kindness altered the perception, which then supported the release of distress.

To nurture is to soften your resistance to what's here and care for the inner harm that resisting causes. The beauty of nurturing is touched when you can see yourself making offers of kindness and care to your own body and mind. Such offerings could be to genuinely forgive or to affirm your basic goodness or that of others. These are experiences to be known through the body, not just in your thoughts. Practice making nurturing offerings to yourself, and then notice how your experiences change, often for the better.

GUIDED PRACTICE FOR **N: NURTURE**
Inquiry: How do I care for this distress?
Practice: In this moment, what's needed that I can offer? What facilitates release and freedom?

Closing Thoughts on RAIN

RAIN supports us in dismantling the construction of racial ignorance and suffering in our mind, body, and heart. We do this not by focusing on our stories about what's happening, but rather by noticing the impact these stories have on us and how this impact leads to distress or freedom. The RAIN practice further helps us recognize where we are at any point in the cycle of misperception—that is, how perceptions feed thoughts and emotions, which feeds beliefs.

In the practice of RAIN, we can begin to notice the subtle and obvious ways we resist the laws of nature—that nothing in life is personal, permanent, or perfect. For example, we can know through our direct experience how thoughts and feelings constantly change. We can experience the mind in distress and how the body is impacted. We can notice that the more fixated or determined we are to have our way, the narrower our view will be and the more trapped we will feel. We can also notice that the discomfort we are experiencing is strengthened or relieved depending on the wisdom we bring to it—the quality of our awareness.

Gary, an African American male I coached, entered a session seething with rage about the killing of unarmed black men by police and the incessant disrespect of black bodies. His rage went on for a good part of the session. His voice was loud and his body animated, and I could feel the heat from his inner scalding.

As he paused in exhaustion, I asked (recognize), "What's happening in your body right now?" He described himself as a volcano ready to explode. He said he was hot and shaky and that his heart was racing.

I asked (allow), "Can you be with it? Can you just be aware of it for now?" He said he could, and I told him to take his time and allow himself to be with the emotions and sensations of being a volcano, ready to explode, hot, shaky, with a racing heart. After a few minutes, he reported that he felt more settled.

I affirmed (allow), "You're right. What's happening is truly horrible. It makes sense that you would be angry." His shoulders shifted downward, his breath continued to settle, his face softened, and he appeared tender, even sad (allow). He continued in silence to recognize and allow.

I then asked (investigate), "How does it feel to be so vulnerable?" This question dazed him and left him speechless. My sense was that in that moment, he had stopped resisting the unbearable reality of the killings and had allowed himself to experience the terror he was trying to escape through anger—the terror that comes from meeting the utter lack of control we have over the hardship that life spits in our faces. His face began to quake, as if the volcano was indeed erupting, but instead of anger, he wept (nurture). I affirmed (allow), "Yes, this too!" Weeping was a more honest response in that moment to his distress and to his release from distress.

When we are at war with or struggle against the energy of our emotions, our minds are zoomed in like a highly focused camera.

We are one with the agitation, boiling and tight in the body. When we zoom in, something is always left out of view. To befriend or nurture our disturbances is to zoom out—to open and allow awareness to be known through a broader lens. To nurture is to speak to our heart and mind with kindness and to become aware without interference, judgment, or wishing things were other than they are.

When we practice in this way, we allow wisdom to permeate the territory of distress. We begin to notice how the nature of racial distress is always changing, often unsatisfactory, and not always a personal affront. We can track more readily what's here and where it leads, and we can choose to relate to our experience more skillfully. For example, we can choose to abandon habitual righteousness and impulses and instead nurture what is wounded into release. Such a practice of care can still be a bumpy ride, but we grow our capacity to glean the wisdom inherent in anxiety and distress—the wisdom of knowing its opposite, release.

We also may begin to notice the subtle ways we disown or dismiss the momentary evidence of freedom—the relief of letting go, that feeling when the mind is not fixated or when a strong sense of self dissolves, when we pause longer in those moments of unconditioned love and spacious awareness. These profound mind states are naturally revealed when we are not at war; we can grow to trust and rest within these mind states.

Gary was highly emotional over what was happening in the world, yet his freedom in that moment came from turning inward, recognizing, allowing, investigating, and nurturing his vulnerability with his own tears. Gary would later share that with RAIN practice, his experiences of inner release strengthened and clarified his outer response to social injustice.

Fundamental to the practice of RAIN is that, over time, our experiences of racial distress can be clearly seen, interrupted, and wisely attended to.

Part 2 Summary

By this point in the journey, we are getting a good taste of what mindfulness practices can do to cool the fires around race and racial distress. Mindfulness practice supports us in examining our relationship to our racial history, beliefs, and impulses. In practice, we investigate the structures of oppression engraved in our mind that are reflected in the world. We sharpen our clarity and strengthen our capacity to be with what we are experiencing internally, without turning away. For example, we can be intimately mindful of wanting instead of having what we want, or we can be mindful of anger without being obsessed with being angry. We can also notice what leads to the inflammation or distress, as well as to the tenderness experienced in moments of release. Fundamentally, we are learning to be present and to see in a different way—a wiser way.

Mindfulness supports us in withdrawing emotional energy from automatic responses and instead invites us to pause, know, and choose how to respond. This pause is powerful because we know both the experience we are having and the fact that it won't kill us. Every time we weather the storm of inner racial discomfort or distress—whether numbness, confusion, or aversion—we are quite literally reprogramming our minds, rewiring our brains toward more stability, well-being, and confidence. Discovering this in a direct way allows us to experience freedom; not freedom as some final destination or permanent state but as a potent moment, a striking glimpse, a homeopathic drop of awareness that is clear, steady, and vast. Just beneath the turbulence of mental torment, this release is accessible and knowable to us through the practice of mindfulness. It's simple, life changing, free, and totally within our control. Do a practice for a period of time. Stay with it. Know for yourself how it supports a more transformed relationship to racial habits of harm.

Being mindful of race is not just about sitting meditation. Mindfulness practice is about changing hearts and, ultimately, living a mindful life. In the next chapters, we extend our mindfulness practice by exploring how we can contribute to a culture of care that embraces race without racism.

Part 3

CULTIVATING A CULTURE OF CARE

~ RECOVERY ~

11

Cultivating Moral Character

*I have a dream that my four little children will one day
live in a nation where they will not be judged by the color
of their skin, but by the content of their character.*

MARTIN LUTHER KING JR.

*A country is only as strong as the people who make it up
and the country turns into what people want it to become. . . .
We made the world we're living in, and we have to make it over.*

JAMES BALDWIN, "Notes for a Hypothetical Novel"

As you become more mindful of race, there is a social responsibility you can't easily escape. For example, if you are doing harm, you feel the need to put a stop to it. If you see someone else doing harm, you feel the need to stop them. If you see systems at work that harm others or that harm the planet, you feel the need to join with others to make sure the harm stops. When you don't act, you are an accomplice to injustice. As Desmond Tutu is said to have advised, "If you are neutral on situations of injustice, you have chosen the side of the oppressor."

To cultivate a culture of care is to be in relationship with humanity with a wise heart. This includes having moral character wrapped in compassion. What I mean by moral character is that we understand and aspire to live by three principles of social harmony:

- Interdependence: This is the practice of remembering that we are part of something larger than our individual selves—a karmic web of humanity—and what we do has impact.

- Compassion: The practice of compassion is a weapon of mass healing.

- Harmlessness: The practice of nonharming in body, speech, and mind is essential for respect and safety.

Ultimately you are not a person, but a focal point where the universe is becoming conscious of itself.
ECKHART TOLLE, spiritual author

One way I have come to understand interdependence, compassion, and harmlessness, particularly in relationship to race, is to see that we all coexist in a vast, skinless body held together by the gravitational pull of Mother Earth's love, shaped in a unique cell suit that we call "self." In this proprioceptive relationship with all existence, each "cell self" represents the whole of existence. As cell selves, we arrive in a variety of colors and races, each serving a purpose that supports the whole—all arising and passing away. In this skinless body is a vast nervous system sensitive to the movement of mind and the beating of hearts. As we become more conscious of our conditioning as racial beings and as one collective force, we enhance the whole of humanity through our lived example. There are notable examples of individuals, cultures, and movements that have influenced—and are still influencing—social well-being.

I'm told that Standing Rock, an indigenous-led resistance movement in North Dakota against intimidating and violent corporate and political forces in favor of the Dakota Pipeline, which violates indigenous treaties and threatens water necessary for life, was organized around an indigenous template for wise choice from several Lakota values. These values include prayer, respect, compassion, honesty, generosity, humility, and wisdom. Such values in action are examples of collective resistance to social injustice that take into consideration all beings and the planet. Standing Rock and the core values lived by the Lakota people of North America reflect care for our kinship, compassion for all, and harmlessness.

Nelson Mandela, the heroic activist against apartheid, was another example. After years of cruelty and harassment, Mandela was sentenced to life in prison and served twenty-seven years, five of which were in hard labor, in a cell less than 10 feet by 8 feet in size. In his years of confinement, Mandela taught the world about nobility, compassion, and the resilience of the human heart. Those of us hungry for hope were deeply inspired by his inner revolution and the people who supported him. Over decades, many of us watched his face and faith grow wise, warm, and content with unwavering grace, determination, and goodness. Through his example and his care for all of us, we saw sacred activism—we saw that it was possible to insist on justice with heart.

Mandela cultivated spiritual maturity and was free in heart and mind well before his physical release from prison in 1990. He knew that resentment is like drinking poison and then hoping it will kill your enemies. The depth of his intention for freedom and unity was refined over time. Shortly after his release, he was elected the first black president of the Republic of South Africa, representing the African National Congress in the first open election in the country's history. Mandela credited his prison experience with teaching him his nonracial outlook and the tactics and strategies that would make him president. A bit of humor also helps—as he once wrote:

"In my country, we go to prison first and then become president." I don't relate Mandela's story to justify the actions of an unjust white supremacy apartheid system, nor do I ignore that as late as 2008, Mandela was on the US terrorism watch list. Instead, I share a bit of his story to illustrate what our hearts and minds are capable of despite our circumstances.

Dr. Martin Luther King Jr. is a profound example of moral character. His long-standing commitment to the civil rights movement was about nonviolence, compassion, and freedom for all races, not just African Americans. I also put Barack Obama in the category of moral character. A few examples include the Affordable Care Act, which provided health insurance to more than twenty million uninsured Americans; his eventual support for the LGBTQ community's fight for marriage equality; his commutation of the sentences of nearly twelve hundred drug offenders to reverse "unjust and outdated prison sentences"; his success in lowering the veteran homeless rate by 50 percent and increasing Department of Veterans Affairs funding; the Healthy Hunger-Free Kids Act to improve school nutrition; his repealing of the military's "Don't Ask, Don't Tell" policy; the Hate Crimes Prevention Act, which makes it a federal crime to assault anyone based on sexual or gender identification; and his nomination of Sonia Sotomayor to the Supreme Court, making her the first Hispanic ever to serve as a justice. Nelson Mandela, Dr. King, President Mandela, and other such leaders were not perfect. Rather they found a way to use their individual power for collective well-being.

It isn't just individuals who embody the principles of interdependence, compassion, and harmlessness. Black Lives Matter began in 2012 after vigilante George Zimmerman was acquitted for murdering Trayvon Martin, a seventeen-year-old unarmed black boy, inside his gated community. *The Guardian* reported that in 2016 alone, across the United States, police killed approximately 258 black people, 34 percent of whom were unarmed black males. That's roughly twenty-two each month or five each week. In an interview on Krista Tippett's onbeing.org, Patrisse Cullors, artist and cofounder of Black Lives Matter, said that this movement is not just about her or even just about all of us. It also brings our ancestors and all people passionate about justice into the movement. She described the movement as healing work, not just about policy:

> You can't policy your racism away. We no longer have Jim Crow laws, but we still have Jim Crow hate. . . . Black Lives Matter is a rehumanizing project. . . . We've forgotten how to imagine black life. Literally, whole human beings have been rendered to die prematurely, rendered to be sick. . . . Our imagination has only allowed for us to understand black people as a dying people. We have to change that. . . . Someone imagined handcuffs; someone imagined guns; someone imagined a jail cell. How do we imagine something different that actually centers on black people, that sees them in the future? Let's imagine something different.

Van Jones, best known as a commentator on Cable News Network, is the founder and president of the Dream Corps, a nonprofit that works to solve America's toughest problems through several initiatives, including reducing the number of people in prisons and jails; building a diverse pipeline for homegrown tech talent; building an inclusive green economy that lifts people out of poverty; and the Love Army, which is working for an America where everyone counts through education, connection, and action.

Such movements are expressions of interdependence, compassion, and doing-no-harm, and they aspire toward racial equity, freedom, and harmony. They show the power of fierce clarity and an understanding of what must be done and how we must go about it to create more social balance and harmony. They demonstrate the need to address systems of oppression with an understanding of our interdependence, along with caring and persistent resistance. We can perhaps sense this transformative twinship from Martin Luther King Jr.'s report to the Southern Christian Leadership Conference in 1967: "Power without love is reckless and abusive, and love without power is sentimental and anemic. Power at its best is love implementing the demands of justice, and justice at its best is love correcting everything that stands against love."

As we turn to our own lives, we don't have to be as grand in our efforts as these political greats. These beloveds, and all who supported them, simply and humbly show us what we are capable of. They leave us to choose for ourselves how we embody moral character. Consider the following principle as you clarify and establish your own practices to cultivate moral character.

Do No Harm

When we are unconscious of how we affect each other, we are more likely to cause harm. However, when nonharming is at the forefront of our awareness, it becomes an anchor, a way of reminding us, moment to moment, to pay attention—to live mindfully.

We all know our habitual impulses as they relate to racial harm and distress. Some of us lash out, some of us hold it all in, and some of us tune out, putting little energy into what distresses us or harms others. How does it feel to be so defended? Can we choose not to respond in habitual ways? Our habitual patterns are good places to begin noticing and renouncing habits of harm and to shift toward caring presence, a condition that is favorable to racial awareness and healing.

For example, what might you discover about yourself if you were to spend the next four hours (or days) not taking anything unless it were offered to you? This includes not initiating and not making anything happen. Not reaching for or being on your various devices. Not asking for anything. Not offering an opinion or judgment or criticism. Not starting conversations or fixing them. Not preparing your food and not purchasing anything. Not reaching for anything. Just receiving. Where would refusing to "do" or "achieve" or "effort" leave you?

Or what might you discover about yourself if you were to renounce comfort for a period of time? My Tibetan teacher of several years, Aba Cecile McHardy, instructed me to practice taking a warm shower and then turning the water from warm to cold without mentally recoiling. This was not intended to be oppressive but more as an experiment in embracing change without preferences—to interrupt the habit of comfort, of having things your way all the time. What thoughts, emotions, or beliefs arise in you at the thought of such a practice? At a minimum, mindfulness is certain to be heightened with such experiments.

Renounce a racial habit of harm and use it as a mindfulness practice for a few hours, a day, or longer. Here are some examples:

- For the next week, I will stop judging the media and notice what I feel in the absence of judging.

- For the next three months, I will only spend money if it is absolutely necessary and notice how it feels to want something without having it.

- For the next week, I will not offer advice unless I am asked.

- For the next two hours, I will allow myself to feel the pain in my lower back without hating that it is here.

Notice how the quality of your awareness is impacted through such a deliberate intention. Once you feel you have an understanding of your relationship with allowing and letting go, renounce another habit and give it your mindful attention.

Renouncing has a very real effect on the function of our brains. Every time we renounce cruelty, greed, righteousness, and hate, we strengthen neuropathways in the middle prefrontal cortex of the brain (for more information, see the discussion of the function of the prefrontal cortex in chapter 4).

By intentionally choosing restraint and knowing it directly, we do less harm to others and ourselves. We become less habituated, impulsive, and anxious because we know what we can do without. We become stronger, more stable, and more full of choice. Most important, we discover what our minds can endure and what our hearts can metabolize.

Get Political

What is notable about the nobles mentioned earlier, as well as the many brave souls who supported them, is that there did not appear to be a distinction between their personal, political, or spiritual lives—they were one and the same. While many of us are challenged with balancing our lives, the truth is there are no lines—we take ourselves everywhere we go, we all get twenty-four hours in a day, and we all make choices.

In the United States, we exist within a federal republic governed by the constitution controlled by the president, the Congress, and federal courts. Many of our ancestors experienced much abuse for the right to vote—insisting on participating in a system that was never made with them in mind. It is now both a right and a privilege that we must take seriously because this system governs every aspect of our day-to-day lives.

Dr. Barbara Riley tells us in her book *Are You Ready for Outrageous Success?* to "Be bothered with the twinges in your gut, when you know something is going on even if you are not totally clear about what . . . Be bothered with the individual and group reactions that are similar to and different than yours." To become politically literate and involved, we need to know the racial biases of our state representatives, governor, mayor, city council, senators, federal and Supreme court officials, and other party officials. We should know the jurisdictions in which we live, the school districts in our state and how they are funded, and how legislation is proposed and laws passed. This also means that when we receive those convoluted and intimidating voting ballots, we must get together with one or two other people and do a bit of research to be better informed of our choices—and then go vote. But we can't stop here. We must also hold those elected accountable for their promises and actions.

When we opt out of this civil responsibility, we become both victims and targets. Poor people and communities of color are often targets of infrastructure neglect, inadequate schools, unhealthy food, crime, racial profiling, water testing, oil drilling, and poor natural disaster response. Political neglect and greed agendas are influenced by our involvement or lack thereof in the political system. To ignore the significance of the political systems that control our lives is to dishonor the work of our ancestors, abuse the generosity of the earth, and work against a culture of care.

The voting process is what put the people who govern our lives into office. If we do not participate in the electoral process, we can't change its dysfunction, and we cannot influence decisions and policies that impact our communities. We may not like the system or trust it, and many of us may not understand how it works, but it is the system we have. And we need to know how it works before we can change it or create a new one. Do a Google search to learn how the system works and get proactively involved. There are people within the community who are politically savvy and resourceful. Seek them out, learn from them, and support them.

Watch Your Spending

A strong branch of racism is rooted in economics. When we become more mindful of how we earn money and how and where we spend it, we can have a tremendous impact on systemic racism. A practice that served us well during the civil rights movement was not to support institutions that discriminated against blacks and other POC. We might also consider whether, when we spend or invest money, we are supporting institutions that fund the prison-industrial complex, weapons, labor exploitation, and other endeavors of harm. It may be difficult to track the money trail and impossible to totally disinvest, but bringing more awareness to our habits of earning and spending can help us discern whether our actions are helping or harming the planet, each other, or ourselves.

We can also assess our habits of excess and assess our level of debt and inquire into when enough is enough. We can explore whether we are spending to feel better or to look good or to have what we need—and at whose expense. There are basic things that all of us need—shelter, food, health care, and water. Many of us have more than we need, while others struggle just to meet their basic needs. Support this imbalance as best you can. Beyond the basics, it's wise to be mindful of when enough is enough.

Spend time redefining the meaning of prosperity with loved ones, and examine how money and other resources are used in your family and community. For example, when we try to comfort our children by showering them with material things, their spiritual growth is interrupted, as is our own. Talk to children about self-reliance, about how less is more; demonstrate how we can show our care for each other without consuming or acquiring more, more, more.

When I asked an activist I work with to give me one example of what a culture of care look likes to her, her response was, "A culture of care is when no one purchases a second home until everyone has shelter." Another civil rights activist stopped eating meat after becoming aware of the ecological harm of meat packaging and the harm to animals. The point is not to beat up on ourselves or others but to align as best we can our spending with our values.

A Word about Wise Speech

Habits of harm are often expressed in our speech. Sometimes our speech, to our surprise and often embarrassment, can tell us what we are really thinking. My mother kept my brother's parrot for several months. I recall visiting her one day, and the parrot began to mimic her one-sided conversation on a recent phone call—her laugh, her criticism, her pace, her tone. She was shocked, and we swore each other to secrecy (until now)! The point here is to ask yourself, "What would your parrot say about your speech?" In Buddhism, we are taught that there are four types of harmful speech:

- Lies—words spoken with the intent of misrepresenting the truth

- Divisive speech—words spoken with the intent of creating rifts between people

- Harsh speech—words spoken with the intent of hurting another person

- Idle chatter—words spoken with no purposeful intent at all

Some of us impulsively speak when we feel racial discomfort. When this happens, we may instead set an intention to pay more attention to our impulse to speak. When we attend to the discomfort that kindles unwise speech, we discover that unwise speech is a habitual strategy that attempts to disguise the anxiety we are experiencing in the moment. Once we give kind attention to the impulses of our speech, we are more likely to uproot the habit of uttering unwise speech.

Speaking wisely is a mindfulness practice. It is an intentional shift from self-interest to self-reflection, and it wakes us up to our responsibility to each other. Nonharming speech can de-escalate racial distress and enable us to feel less defensive and more hopeful. Pick one area of wise speech to pay attention to for a certain period. Notice how it supports inner stability, well-being, and confidence and how it supports more care in your interactions.

Poet David Whyte offered a fresh perspective through his concept of a "conversational identity." The idea is that we are constantly changing and evolving, always in the middle of something; therefore, our relationships should be fluid, more conversational, where we are not completing the work but rather beginning the conversation. He explained that such conversations should reflect a language of affection in order to enter the hearts of others. Offering a language of affection is the spirit of wise speech, where, with each encounter, we are kind, present, and curious about the human life that stands before us. We should speak the truth respectfully, in ways that lead to connection and wise action.

Make Kindness a Priority

Kindness requires effort. The untrained mind inclines naturally toward fear and often ill will. The kindness or metta practice I offered in chapter 8 relieves our racial distress by cultivating goodwill. It supports us in consciously shifting from ill will to non–ill will to goodwill. With practice, we experience warmth and ease and discover the spaciousness we need to make wise choices. Kindness cannot be left out of the moral equation. In this practice, we invite the heart to open to warmth and to genuine acceptance, and we prime the mind to embrace racial fear and distress in an atmosphere of non-hatred. This is a fundamental practice for cultivating moral character. Don't leave home without it!

Concluding Thoughts

Moral character requires that we use the challenges of racial ignorance, injustice, and distress to sharpen our awareness of our interdependence, the need for compassion, and the power of nonharming. How this occurs for each of us is as diverse as the races, but what is core is that we must start—even if it feels impossible or even if we don't finish in our lifetime. We must own our membership in a collective humanity and realize again and again that what must be done must be done for the benefit of current and future generations.

Social change that tugs at the hearts of the oppressed has historically required mass movements, and this necessity will likely not change in our lifetime. However, what can and does change is the quality of heart and clarity of mind we bring to it. This is the work of being mindful of race.

12

Compassion Practice

*Just as parents care for their children,
you should bear in mind the whole universe.*

DŌGEN, Zen master

*Compassion is the keen awareness
of the interdependence of all things.*

THOMAS MERTON, American Catholic writer and theologian

The heart's nature is to care, but our arteries get clogged with racial stressors like anger, fear, impulsivity, pity, over-whelm, and despair. We become preoccupied with our own lives and fixated on our own views and beliefs. Our challenge is to widen our circles of compassion so that nothing and no one is left out of our care. In this chapter, I offer a number of sitting practices that support us in cultivating the heart of compassion. Compassion in action is explored in the next several chapters. Here, I first want to strengthen our capacity to open and rest in our wise hearts.

The word *compassion* literally means to suffer with others, to feel what they feel, and, I would add, to feel without papancha—without adding layers of distress. In Hebrew, the word for compassion is derived from the word for "womb." Thus, we can discern that to have compassion is to be like every mother is to her own child.

I recently gave a dharma talk to a predominantly white meditation community. After a thirty-minute silent meditation, I had everyone state their name with a spacious breath. This ritual is intended to provide a sense of connection and belonging. As everyone finished, I offered a few names of people who were present in my mind but no longer with us:

Rumain Brisbon, 34, Phoenix, AZ	killed December 2, 2014
Tamir Rice, 12, Cleveland, OH	killed November 22, 2014
Akai Gurley, 28, Brooklyn, NY	killed November 20, 2014
Kajieme Powell, 25, St. Louis, MO	killed August 19, 2014
Ezell Ford, 25, Los Angeles, CA	killed August 11, 2014
Dante Parker, 36, San Bernardino, CA	killed August 12, 2014
Michael Brown, 18, Ferguson, MO	killed August 9, 2014
John Crawford III, 22, Beavercreek, OH	killed August 5, 2014
Eric Garner, 43, New York, NY	killed July 17, 2014
Jonathan Ferrell, 24, Charlotte, NC	killed September 14, 2013

I then said to the group, "These are just a few of the names of unarmed African American men, women, and children killed by police over the past several months, and I'm Ruth King, their Mother."

It was a heartfelt evening in which we explored the epidemic of violence that was infesting many of our communities near and far, and we discussed how to stay intimately present with an open heart.

Undoubtedly, one person on that list would have been too many, and it would not surprise me to know that some of you reading this book have had experiences of such senseless loss or violence at the hands of those in power. To you I offer compassion for continuing to heal. For the many others, however, who can turn away, I invite you—as I invited the practitioners that evening— not only to consider the fact that these killings occurred and continue to occur but also to feel into the heartbreak of these acts with compassion and to touch the raw reality that many of us live with.

- Suppose the common violence toward and killing of dark bodies were happening toward your own children or dear ones? How would you feel?

- Imagine stepping into the skin of the mothers, fathers, sisters, brothers, children, or families of one of these men, women, or children. What do you experience in your body, mind, and heart?

- Consider that your mother, father, sister, brother, son, or daughter is one of the people on this list. What feelings or thoughts arise? How would you feel if there was no indictment for the police officers who killed your loved one under conditions when such an act could have clearly been avoided?

- Imagine you are the mother or father, son or daughter of the police who did the killing? What do you experience in your body, mind, and heart?

- Notice from your bodily sensations what actions feel urgent. How clear are you about taking those actions?

- How would you feel if you had done everything humanly possible to seek justice to no avail? What would you feel and be inclined to do?

- What are you feeling in your heart, body, and mind as you sit with this contemplation? Are you on fire? Numb? Sad? Bored? Indifferent?

As we commit ourselves to being mindful of race, we begin to notice the pervasive depth of racial harm and injustice in our immediate lives and throughout the world. The constellations of harm become more vivid. We also feel the soreness and tenderness that comes with such awareness and notice the habitual ways our body and mind defend against it. One client shared this reflection:

> When I think about forgiving my mom who was a proud racist and so hateful toward me, I feel lighter and more spacious. Then a sharp muscle tightens around my heart as if to say "hell no" to the vulnerability I'm feeling. I can't quite articulate what

it means in my heart to let go, and why I have such muscle memory to hold onto so fiercely, but I'm okay, even curious.

We see that habits of harm are not necessarily our making—they are ways the body naturally attempts to protect us from perceived threat. By recognizing our distress in such moments and attending to it with care, we become more sensitive and compassionate. Such tenderizing, over time, supports us in knowing the delicate needs of others and the necessity of responding with care. We are all hardwired with racial conditioning, and we all unfold differently. Compassion supports this process.

Bearing witness to racial suffering without turning away, we discover our humanity, our innate kinship. When we are touched in direct ways, we begin to move through the world with more awareness and sensitivity, ensuring that no one else experiences such pain again. Poet and songwriter Naomi Shihab Nye's poem "Kindness" exemplifies this idea:

> Before you learn the tender gravity of kindness
> you must travel where the Indian in a white poncho
> lies dead by the side of the road.
> You must see how this could be you,
> how he too was someone
> who journeyed through the night with plans
> and the simple breath that kept him alive.

In my dharma talk, I ended with this: "The next time you hear of a brown person being killed by anyone, stay present and say to yourself: 'Oh my, another one of Ruth's children has been killed.' Then check in with your own heart to determine the appropriate response."

Compassion to Ourselves

Compassionate towards yourself,
you reconcile all beings in the world.

LAO-TZU, *Tao Te Ching*

Compassion is the wish that everyone, without exception, is free from pain and suffering and its causes. Yet, the weight of racial suffering can be heavy on the body, heart, and mind. Most of us want our distress to go away without caring for it.

Compassion practice serves as an anticoagulant to such burdens. With practice, we experience more inner circulation—more flow, lightness, and openness. There is more space to soften, to forgive, and to receive all that life offers. We begin to realize there is more love in our heart than anything else—we're just not in the habit of relying on it.

The following guided meditation was inspired by the teachings of my dharma sister, Catherine McGee of Gaia House, in Devon, England.

GUIDED COMPASSION PRACTICE FOR OURSELVES

To begin, take a position of relaxed awareness and begin to connect with your own body and the larger body—earth—holding you. Bring awareness to the breath moving through your body, entering and exiting as the breath joins with the larger element air—air moving in, air moving through, air moving out. Take a few moments to rest and savor the presence of the earth and air—always with you.

Next, invite a trio of protection to surround you. You might imagine a benefactor sitting right behind you—someone who is there for you with wise guidance; on the right of you is someone you deeply care for; and on your left is a younger, more innocent version of yourself. Imagine them sitting close enough for you to feel their warmth and care, as if their presence were wrapping you in a warm blanket. Allow every cell in your body to be bathed by this compassionate regard as you thank them for being with you. Feel the warmth from the earth and the mutual regard flowing between the four of you.

Take time to linger and rest in this initial practice. Stay present to your body and breath as you offer this compassion first to yourself, then to a challenging person or situation, and finally to all beings.

Bring to mind an aspect of yourself that needs your compassion. Maybe a part of you that has been suffering directly or that has been impacted by racial harm. Allow it to reveal itself naturally. This aspect of yourself may be clear or vague, younger or older, past or present—it does not matter. Gently invite it to come close, to sit before you, and to join your trio of protection.

Allow yourself to be touched by its presence. Welcome it, saying, "I care, I care," and ask it to tell you its story. For example, it may want to tell you how and why it feels ashamed, enraged, numb, lonely, abandoned, clueless, in hiding, sad, anxious, indifferent, wounded, determined, punishing, weary, or afraid. Listen with your entire body as you feel the support of Mother Earth beneath you and your trio of protection surrounding you.

Breathing into the center of your chest, allow yourself to be touched by the suffering you are experiencing. Feel the heat, darkness, heaviness, sharpness, sadness, stuckness, despair, fear, or whatever else is present in your direct experience. Don't be afraid. It won't break your heart; it will open your heart. Breathing out, feel the coolness, brightness, and lightness. Sense any freshness and relief as you repeat these statements to yourself silently, feeling the good intention behind them:

- Welcome, dear one. I see your pain. You don't need to be afraid. I will take care of you.

- I'm here. I care about your suffering. I will stay with you. I will breathe with you.

- It is my wish to care for you wholeheartedly right now, for as long as it takes.

- May you be soothed. May you be healed.

- I'm sorry you have been ignored and kept away. I will stay with you now and care for you.

- I may not always know how to show you that I care, but I am here for you.

- When you feel deep sorrow, hopelessness, and despair, I will stay with you. I will breathe with you.

- When it is necessary for you to hide, I will wait patiently by your door.

- May you be soothed. May you be healed.

- When you scream and are on fire with rage, I will stay with you until the fire subsides.

- When you appear hardened and impenetrable, I will stand beside you.

- May you be soothed. May you be healed.

- When you share your most humiliating or murderous accounts, I will not turn away. I will stay with you. I will breathe with you.

- May you be soothed. May you be healed.

Take your time repeating a few or all of these phases or create your own. Focus your attention at the chest or heart area as you breathe in and breathe out. Stay present.

> *Don't surrender your loneliness so quickly.*
> *Let it cut more deep.*
> *Let it ferment and season you*
> *as few human or even divine ingredients can.*
> HAFIZ, Persian poet

Notice the movements between the heart opening and closing and welcome both the resistance and its release as it is experienced in the body. Breathe in through all of your pores the wish to relieve pain and fear. Breathe out so that you have more space to linger and rest with ease. Repeat the phrases slowly and quietly, feeling your sincere intention to relieve suffering.

Finally, allow this part of you to fade away. Notice the quality of heart and mind that remains, paying particular attention to the resonance of compassion. Abide in whatever silence, stillness, and solace is present.

Compassion for a Difficult Person, Situation, or Institution

Fact: There are racial groups with power who are ignorant, righteous, and dangerous and who are doing intentional and systematic harm to other races. This harsh reality is not likely to vanish in our lifetime. Wisdom and compassion are both required. We can ask, for example, "How do I fight for racial justice with heart and without doing harm to others or to myself?" or "How do I respond to the ignorance in the world—those people, situations, and institutions that I can't control?" These questions bring wise inquiry into the heart of our sitting practice. The simple yet often difficult answer is to respond with compassion.

I once came across a wise passage though have been unable to find its source, but its meaning still holds true: "It is not our work to force someone's growth to our liking. It is the work of love to admire the beauty before you, to give people a sense of safety to unfold. To keep each other company when drowning in anguish until the wave can balance out and our feelings can once again live in us."

I resonate with this message as a core value, but at the same time, I can hear some of you saying, "Bullshit! We must force; love can wait!" I believe we can fight with firm love. Many of us as parents know this kind of love when we must set a firm boundary with our children to insist that they are not harmed or that they do no harm. We hope that our children learn from such firm love. When we use our power to enforce without love, we may have superficial change but not transformation. Transformation requires wise love—love rooted in nonharming and an understanding of our interdependence and the power of compassion. Wise love may not result in the outcome we seek, but it does not work against it.

Nora, a white woman I coached for several months and an experienced meditator, came to a session in high distress over a list of wrongdoings by President Donald Trump. I invited her to close her eyes and settle in by giving her attention to the exhales of her breath. Once her breathing slowed and her full body appeared to be breathing, I said, "I want you to bring the image of President Trump into the center of your heart and mind and tell me, as you look at him, how you feel and what you want to say or do." Nora replied:

> I feel agitated and nervous. I'm trying to stay away from my head, so I'm scanning my body for a safe place. Fear is present. Something feels like a threat. Yes, I feel endangered—afraid for myself and for others. I can see him—Trump. My chest and the palms of my hands are hot and sweaty. I want to push Trump into a chair, put my hands on his shoulders, and put tape over his mouth. I want to say to him: "You cannot move until you understand the impact of your action and your responsibility. Until you get this, you cannot be the president." [long pause] I want to hold him here in this room until he gets it, and he may never get it. I want to protect him from himself, like a parent would do with an out-of-control child. I envision many wise and caring people surrounding him, to contain him with compassion, and to heal him and all of us. I can feel my spine more. I'm sitting up straighter. I feel clear and openhearted. I'm clear about what needs to happen. He needs to be contained because he cannot contain himself, yet he is an ominous threat. I need to contain him, not attack him, but to not let him hurt others. I want to pour love on him until he changes, and he may not change. Maybe he stays here in this room for the rest of his life. And maybe he wouldn't change, but everyone else would be safe. I will pray for him, for his well-being and his peace—for without this, he does not have a chance to feel for others. And I will do everything in my power to align with others to make sure his harm stops.

When Nora opened her eyes, she shared that she felt powerful, centered, and clear.

Nora's experience is a strong example of the fierce heart of compassion. Her clarity came from presence. She was able not only to track what was arising in her mind but also to notice the impact it was having on her body. The aim of this exercise was not for Nora to seek a way to literally restrain the president in a room; rather, this exercise allowed her to feel the power of her own restraint and compassion and to align with her intent. Compassion practice motivates wise action.

Some communities have created healing rituals or ceremonies that support a compassionate response toward an individual's wrongdoing. These ceremonies often involve the entire community that has been affected directly or indirectly by the wrongdoing, and it is a way to show firm compassion and belonging. My teacher, Jack Kornfield, shared a story of one such ritual from the Babemba tribe of South Africa:

> When a person acts irresponsibly or unjustly, he is
> placed in the center of the village, alone and unfettered.
> All work ceases, and every man, woman, and child in
> the village gathers in a large circle around the accused
> individual. Then each person in the tribe, regardless
> of age, begins to talk out loud to the accused, one at a
> time, about all the good things the person in the center
> of the circle has done in his lifetime. Every incident,
> every experience that can be recalled with any detail and
> accuracy is recounted. All his positive attributes, good
> deeds, strengths, and kindnesses are recited carefully and
> at length. No one is permitted to fabricate, exaggerate, or
> be facetious about his accomplishments or the positive
> aspects of his personality. The trial ceremony often
> lasts several days and does not cease until everyone is

drained of every positive comment he can muster about the person in question. At the end, the tribal circle is broken, a joyous celebration takes place, and the person symbolically and literally is welcomed back into the tribe.

Reflect for a few moments. Close your eyes and imagine how it would feel to have your wrongdoings responded to in this wise way. Imagine sitting in the center of that circle and hearing only good things about you for hours. What affect does it have on your heart, body, and mind? Linger here for a few breaths. Now, imagine how it would feel to partake in such a ceremony. Next, imagine someone who has been harmful to you sitting in the center of that circle. Imagine remembering all the goodness you can recall about that person. What affect does it have on your heart, body, and mind? Again, linger and rest in this reflection. When you feel ready, you may open your eyes.

Repeating this exercise is a practice of self-compassion and compassion for others. You can bring anyone into the center of your mind and flood them with compassion. You can also place yourself in the center of your heart and make kind and genuine offerings to yourself. You can also gather with others to create compassion ceremonies that strengthen community well-being and healing.

GUIDED COMPASSION PRACTICE
FOR A DIFFICULT PERSON

To begin this compassion practice, take a few moments to settle into the body, reestablishing your trio of protection. Once you feel settled, bring to mind a difficult person, situation, or institution that you feel is doing racial harm out of ignorance, greed, or hatred. Invite them to enter into your trio of protection and sit before you. Determine whether you want them sitting closer or farther away. Notice how it feels inside your body and heart to have them clearly seated before you as you set an intention to stay present to their presence.

When you are ready, and only when you are ready, invite them to tell you their stories of suffering—how they came to be strong in their views and determined in their actions. Look closely. Notice what is obvious as well as what is nuanced or subtle. Imagine stepping into their skin as they tell the story; feel what it might be like to hold their views and beliefs. How you feel in your body is likely how it feels in their body.

Allow this to be a time of noninterference—simply let the person, situation, or institution be as they are and say what they need to say. Welcome the suffering that is there with awareness and care, being open to hearing and feeling the unexpected. Stay with your body sensations without acting on the impulse to engage, be at war, or figure anything out. Allow your entire body to be an open ear and rely on your trio of protection for grounded warmth and support.

Breathing in, allow yourself to be touched by their stories. Feel the heat, darkness, righteousness, heaviness, sadness, hopelessness, stuckness, despair, fear, or whatever else is present as you allow their suffering—a suffering that, in this moment, you both share. Use your own relationship to suffering to recognize their suffering, knowing that, more than anything, in this moment, your care is precious and needed. Breathe out coolness, brightness, and lightness, a sense of freshness and reprieve, as you repeat the following phrases, offering your sincere wish for the relief of their suffering:

- I'm here. I care about your suffering.

- I am holding your pain and sorrow with compassion.

- May you be soothed. May you be healed.

- May your sadness, pain, and sorrow be eased.

- May your fears dissolve.

- I'm sorry you have been harmed, ignored, and dismissed. I will stay with you. I will breathe with you.

- I may not know how to support you in the best way, but it is my wish to do so.

- May you be soothed. May you be healed.

- May suffering be a kind teacher.

- May you hold yourself in compassion.

- May you be soothed. May you be healed.

Take your time repeating a few or all of these phases or create your own. Repeat the phrases slowly and quietly, feeling the spaces in between your words. Focus your attention at the chest or heart area as you breathe in and breathe out.

Breathe in the sincere wish to listen and take away all of their suffering. Breathe out that they may be well and unafraid and have more space to respond to racial suffering with more care. Feel these prayers coming in and going out through all of your pores.

Again, notice the movement between the heart opening and closing; welcome both the resistance and its release as it is experienced in the body. Breathe in the wish to relieve pain and fear. Breathe out so that you have more space to linger and rest with ease. Repeat the phrases slowly and quietly.

Finally, allow the difficult person, situation, or institution to fade away, seeing them leave with more strength and humility. Notice the quality of heart and mind that remains as they leave, paying particular attention to the resonance of compassion. Rest in whatever silence, stillness, and solace is present.

Offering Compassion to the Suffering in the World

The skeletal shape of oppression—dominance and subordination—whether it is racial, political, or religious, can be recognized throughout the United States and in most parts of the world, including Bosnia, Myanmar, Syria, Palestine, Canada, Haiti, North Korea, Brazil, Australia, Africa, and India, just to name a few. Countless group identities suffer from daily indignities including class and gender inequity, sexual orientation and abilities inequity, structural racism, removal from their land, restrictions from entering their land, being warehoused in prisons or controlled by a militarized police force, being snatched for sex trafficking, and living in intentionally created poverty zones that have existed for generations. And then there is the brown body of Mother Earth herself—our superior mother, who gives birth to all that sustains us. She is at risk and rebelling, like other dark bodies, against abuse and exploitation. All are in need of compassion, care, and protection, including those who, knowingly or unknowingly, harm.

GUIDED COMPASSION PRACTICE FOR ALL

To practice offering compassion to all beings, begin by establishing mindfulness as discussed in the preceding guided compassion practice. Breathing in, allow yourself to be touched by the racial suffering in our families, communities, nations, the world, and the planet. Feel the heat, darkness, heaviness, sadness, hopelessness, despair, fear, or whatever else is present as you allow this suffering to be known—a suffering we all share. Breathe out coolness, brightness, and lightness, a sense of freshness and well-being, as you repeat the following phrases, offering your sincere wish for the relief of the world's suffering:

- I care about your suffering.

- May all sentient beings be soothed and healed.

- I'm sorry you have been harmed, exploited, ignored, and hated. I care about your suffering.

- May all sentient beings be safe from inner and outer danger.

- I may not know how to show that I care, but I am doing what I can to make a difference.

- May all sadness, pain, and sorrow be eased.

- I hold all beings, without exception, in compassion.

- May all beings be free from fear.

- May all beings feel my care and meet racial difficulties with courage and kindness.

- May all beings be free from pain and sorrow.

- May all beings be free from racial suffering.

- May suffering be a great teacher.

- May all beings be soothed and be healed.

Breathe in for all of us, and breathe out for all of us. Breathe in the wish to take away all the racial pain and suffering in the world. Breathe in the suffering so that all sentient beings can be well and have more space to relax, open, and heal. Breathing out, feel the qualities of compassion being released through all of your pores and out into the world for the benefit of all sentient beings. Take as much time as you need as you feel the goodness of your intention to relieve suffering.

End the meditation by thanking your trio of protection for their care—your benefactor, your dear one, and your little one. Allow them to fade away, leaving you with the blessing that you are safe, content, healthy, and at ease. Continue to abide in their blessings for a while; then allow this experience to inspire what you do next.

Concluding Thoughts on Compassion Practice

We practice compassion for those who are racially ignorant, hateful, remorseful, and unforgiving—and we can include ourselves in this lineup. We discover through this practice that we can do more than beat up others and ourselves for how things are. As we practice, we can recognize ourselves in the suffering of others, even in its grand disguises. For example, when someone strikes out at us, we know we have options. We can strike back, or we can pause and tune into the suffering that is being displayed. We can empathize by recalling a time when we, too, struck out at someone; we know what that's like internally and the hurtful impact it has on others. From this mature reflection, we can respond with more empathy. Sometimes it takes a raised voice to make a point. For example, we can scream "hell no" and set a firm boundary, while also holding ourselves and others in compassion. In our firmness, we don't leave our heart out of the mix, and we acknowledge to ourselves that harming others intentionally or righteously is not an option. Responding to racial distress in this way is a movement towards care—more healing than harming.

When we practice compassion in our daily sitting practice and throughout the day, we let go by softening the tightness in our own heart and mind. With practice, we recognize and allow our own ignorance and innocence and that of others, and we nurture both the heartbreak of racial suffering and its release.

Life can feel unbearable if we are afraid of getting our hearts broken again and again from the pervasiveness and pressures of racial ignorance and distress. However, when we maintain a consistent compassion practice, we discover that, although the ego can't hold both hate and love at the same time, the wise heart can. Compassion practice is a way to awaken the benevolence that is inherent in all of us, no matter how cruel or cold the world appears to be.

To be mindful of race is to touch into the terror of fear, vulnerability, and how we feel when we can't control others or control what is happening in the moment. But we also touch so much more, including our deep wish for safety, happiness, and freedom for all beings.

13

The Wake-Up Call

Racial Affinity Groups

t is not enough to think we can simply get a racially diverse group in one room and "hash it out"—many of us have been there and done that to no avail. We show up with good intentions, but we are afraid, unclear, unskilled, angry, and cautious, all of which get in the way of us connecting and being real. And with regularity, we put our foot in our mouths and then become frustrated or belligerent—or just shut down.

There is no shift in consciousness around race without the grit that relating to each other makes possible. However, given the unintended harm caused from unawareness and cumulative impact when we gather across races, we need a different way, or perhaps an alternative way, to explore the ignorance and innocence of our racial conditioning and racial character with those of our same race. I recommend racial affinity groups (RAGs) as an ongoing forum for investigating and transforming our individual and collective habits of harm.

In a RAG, we put ourselves in intentional spaces with people of our same race, where we can be safe enough to be vulnerable, challenged, and unedited; to examine the stories we have been told and the stories we tell ourselves; to lean toward what is unfamiliar and away from what is habitual; and to understand what is difficult to acknowledge, feel, and attend to within us and among us as a racial group.

RAGs offer a structure of inquiry and can address many needs. They support us in exploring what has been forbidden, forgotten, and unhealed. For example, in a RAG, white people can discover together their group identity. They can cultivate racial solidarity and compassion and support each other in sitting with the discomfort, confusion, and numbness that often accompany white racial awakening. They can also discern white privilege and its impact without the aid of or dependence on POC. White people who have formed RAGs report that they recognized their collective commonality and shared history, as well as the impact that their privilege has had on other races and on each RAG member.

While many POC may not need an affinity group to help them relate to their racial group membership, they may need to explore the diversity that exists among POC and across POC without having the distraction of having to educate white people on whiteness and its harm. A habitual focus on white people can distract POC from knowing themselves as a diverse body. Exploring this tender territory in a RAG can be a wholesome alternative to expecting white people at large, who often are not aware of being racial beings, to relieve the intense distress experienced by POC.

In a RAG, whether for POC or for whites, we have the opportunity to share our experiences and histories, examine our impulses, reinterpret meaning, and see clearly our role in racial harming and healing. Such groups support us in being more vulnerable and in grieving the ignorance, shame, and disgrace that often accommodate racial inquiry.

A RAG brings us into clear intention and is a critical step in developing, from the inside out, racial intimacy, literacy, and skillfulness. To separate into same-race groups, in this sense, is not intended to divide us but rather to leverage the fact that, in relative reality, we are racially divided. In a RAG, we use separation to more deeply understand this conditioning.

RAGs are fundamental to transforming habits of harm and to healing racism. Regardless of how you identify racially, no one is exempt from the need to intimately examine racial conditioning.

Forming a Racial Affinity Group

To begin, invite two to seven people of your race to join you in raising self-awareness and literacy for the purpose of reducing racial harm and increasing racial harmony from the inside out. Most groups have reported that to stay focused on race, it is helpful to select people similar to your racial identity and/or gender. For example, all white groups, or all black women, or all white men, or all white women, or all black men, or mixed-race groups, or immigrant groups, etc. I encourage groups to make a minimum of a yearlong commitment, meeting at least monthly for no less than three hours. The following structure could be useful in your RAG meeting:

- 30-minute silent meditation

- 60-minute sharing/discussion

- 15-minute gratitude and reflections

- 15-minute silent meditation

- 15-minute next steps discussion

Group tasks should be shared or rotated. Many RAGs also include meal sharing. Tasks may include choosing a meeting location, sending reminders, determining meeting topics, leading guided meditations, guiding discussions, and scheduling. Sharing responsibility supports group kinship and cohesion.

Make coming together as simple as possible. In the first few meetings, as the group is still forming, I encourage members to simply meditate together, share intentions, and explore how to best support each other's commitments. Initially, the focus should be on listening and connecting.

Before engaging in the racial inquiry questions that follow, however, RAG members should have met consistently and feel ready to commit to deeper inquiry. Although the inquiry questions will likely deepen group cohesion, it is a higher-risk intervention as a starting place. Take the time for the RAG to establish consistency and stability among its members before taking more vulnerable risks.

The intention of a RAG is to be mindful and to create a safe place to explore racial ignorance, aversion, and urgency. Discussion topics should be focused on understanding group member racial conditioning at the individual and group identity levels. The group should not focus on addressing social issues or learning about other races. Rather, RAG members are to discover intimately their relationship with their own race. Some groups have studied various books or explored genealogy, family programing, racial trauma, or history museums. The idea is not to have a tight script but to have a firm inner focus and safe container for deepening understanding.

Waking up together in a RAG is not insignificant. The intimacy of a small group makes the emotions and vulnerability more intense. Our experiences will fluctuate from being aware that we are unskilled, to having what we are unaware of pointed out, to noticing and even being surprised by our own goodness. When we add the shame and embarrassment that leaks out when we discover what we don't know, or when we say or do something that exposes our imperfections, ignorance, aversion, or selfishness, we may want to withdraw from the group to avoid embarrassment and discomfort. For these reasons, I offer the following guidelines, which have been helpful in forming and sustaining a RAG.

- Attend your RAG eager to listen, learn, share, and be heard.

- Commit to your RAG. Inconsistent attendance or distractions by outside interests negatively affect safety and the quality of disclosure.

- Throughout your RAG gathering, maintain respect for the humanness of each person participating.

- At the beginning of each meeting, commit to confidentiality, pledging that whatever is said in the RAG stays in the RAG.

- Only the person sharing should speak. There are no interruptions or cross-talking. As the group becomes more stable, engagement or dialogue can be added.

- When sharing, you determine the level of disclosure and vulnerability you will express.

- When speaking, take your time. Speak slowly and experience your words.

- When someone else is sharing, pay attention to what is being said and recognize the courage it takes to say it.

- Relax and release expectations. No opinions, judgments, or dislikes are to be expressed (verbally or nonverbally) toward the person sharing.

- Tune into your own experience—how you are being touched and shaped by the gifts offered. Be curious about your inner experience, not just your thoughts.

- No questions should be asked of the person sharing. Listeners should receive what is being said as a gift that is being slowly unwrapped. You can't know what the gift will be until it has opened, and it is always opening. Maintain compassionate patience and curiosity.

- While gentle, clarifying questions can be useful, listeners are not to probe, argue, seek agreement, or invoke anger or passive forms of retaliation. Nor should listeners speak of their own story when someone is sharing. Do not in any way take attention away from the person speaking.

- When you feel uneasy, turn inward to how you feel, while also staying present to what you are sharing or to what is being shared.

- At any time during your RAG, when things become too intense or if you feel uneasy, you can request that the group pause in silence together. Stillness and breathing may be all that are required. You may also track your experience in silence by applying the RAIN inquiry (recognize, allow, investigate, and nurture). Or, if the person speaking is willing, they may track their experience out loud while others bear compassionate witness.

- Should you want to talk about something that was said during your RAG once the group time has ended, ask permission of the person before engaging.

- Whenever you are expressing your concern, make presence and deepening the relationship a priority.

REFLECTIONS AT THE CLOSE OF RAG
- How does it feel to sit together and talk about race?
- How do we support each other in waking up and healing?
- What I hope can happen for all of us as we continue this work is . . .

After a RAG gathering has ended, you may find it helpful to reflect on how you feel about the inquiry itself. For example, you might sit quietly or journal your thoughts on the following questions:

- How am I doing right now? What's the mood of my mind and heart? Am I sad, frightened, hopeful or hopeless, enraged, ashamed. . .?
- How do I feel about what I am discovering?
- What keeps me committed to being mindful of race and transforming racism?
- What can I appreciate about my life and my choices today? What can I celebrate about the life of others?

Racial Inquiry Questions

The following questions might be helpful reflections for your mindfulness sitting practice or to be explored within your RAG. Spend some time each day reflecting on a question or two from the list that follows. Some of the questions may serve as a stimulus, and others may invite you to do a bit of research outside of your sitting or RAG practice. Still other questions may arouse more questions. Use these questions as a mindfulness practice to become more aware of how you are relating to the questions themselves. Drop them directly into stillness and notice how you experience them. Notice whether the question brings you distress or release. There is no rush to get through the list or anywhere other than here. And feel free to create your own questions.

Each time you begin, take three intentional deep breaths, focusing on your exhale. Start with a body scan, inviting any physical or mental tension to soften as you bring kind attention to each area of the body, starting at the top of the head, moving slowly and with ease throughout the body down to your toes. Allow yourself to experience this softening on the inside of the body—not just the sounds of your words but also the actual experience of the movement of awareness through your own body. As you feel more settled, imagine your mind resting in your entire body. Take a few breaths here to simply linger and rest in awareness. When you feel settled, contemplate the following questions with as much ease as possible. As you explore these questions and begin to notice tension in the body or mind, take a few breaths and reground in the body before returning to the question.

EXPLORING INDIVIDUAL IDENTITY

- Why do you believe matters of race are still matters of concern throughout the world today?

- What traumas marked your youth? How do they impact and inform your life today?

- As a child, what were you taught about being a racial human being? What were you not taught?

- When did you first discover you were a race? What circumstances surrounded this discovery?

- What are the roots of your racial lineage? Given your lineage, what has your race gained or lost throughout the generations? How have these gains or losses influenced your racial views today?

- As you reflect on your racial history, what is disturbing to recall?

- Where in your life do you feel numb, shut down, dismembered, disrespected, or disconnected? What is your earliest memory of feeling this way? What events or circumstances do you believe gave birth to these experiences? What do you believe such feelings keep you from knowing?

- What views did your ancestors, elders, parents, or caretakers have about race? How did their views impact you? In what ways were/are your views similar or different?

- What elders or caretakers are still alive in your family? Would you be willing to have an open conversation with them about race? If not, why not? If so, what would you want to ask them? What would you want to tell them? In what ways might you "keep the peace" and stay with the status quo?

- How has racial fear, shame, anger, or guilt gotten in the way of you having more intimate relationships with your own race? With other races?

- What has your relationship to your own race kept you from experiencing, knowing, or understanding about other races?

- What recurring hardships do you personally experience as they relate to race and to racism?

EXPLORING RACIAL GROUP IDENTITY

- What racial identities or ethnicities have shaped how you have come to know yourself as a race?

- What personal beliefs or actions—past and present—could have jeopardized your membership in your racial group? What risk can you take today that you could not take in the past?

- Under what circumstances do you notice race? Talk about race? What thoughts, feelings, and emotions are commonly stimulated in these situations?

- What role did your ancestors play in racial oppression and racial healing?

- What's racially unfinished, forgotten, or ungrieved in your racial lineage? What impact might reclaiming this unfinished business have on social harmony?

- What has membership in your racial group protected you from knowing, experiencing, or trusting about other racial groups? Why was this believed to be necessary? What's at risk in challenging such protections?

- What do you have in common with others in your racial affinity group? What diversity exists among you?

- In what ways do you feel you need to distinguish yourself from your racial group? Why is this important?

- What beliefs do you have about other racial groups that create inner distress? How do these beliefs impact your relationship to your own race and to racism?

- What questions about race do you want to ask of your racial affinity group members?

- What are you reluctant to share or speak out loud with members of your own race? With other races?

- What can you talk about or own about your racial history that you couldn't talk about in the past (the past could be earlier today)?

- What stops any one race from knowing another race?

- How do you as an individual and as a RAG work with members of your race to raise racial awareness and challenge habits of harm?

In this mindfulness inquiry, it is common to experience distrust, embarrassment, and fear when sharing personal and racial information, or to collude in silence and presumed solidarity to maintain membership within your RAG. These feelings can trigger the impulse to strike out, shut down, or remain superficial or guarded in our interactions. Don't be discouraged! Choosing to remain engaged without judgment or fear often results in a more honest exchange and deeper connection.

Remember, engaging these questions within a RAG is not the end game; rather, it prepares us to better engage across racial differences. In this inquiry of compassion, we are strengthening our commitment to nonharming and learning how to be honest and to share the weight of racial ignorance and distress among our own race. As self-awareness grows, we begin to extend this same care, curiosity, and respect to everyone we encounter within and outside of our RAG. Such intentional acts contribute to a culture of care.

14

Talking about
What Disturbs You

n this chapter, we explore how to talk about what disturbs you with people in your own race and with people of a different race. Talking about race can feel discouraging. Most of us who have been in racial discussions—and survived them—can share weary stories and war wounds. Too often we are left feeling battered, bruised, hopeless, and powerless. Feeling vulnerable and unsafe, we separate, unable to manage the anxiety that often comes with relating. We retreat to our corners—a smaller and more deficient world of false comforts. This separation shuts down the opportunity to become more self-aware as racial beings and more knowledgeable of our impact on each other and the communities where we live.

The following is a mindfulness practice of talking about what disturbs you. This practice is strengthened when you are maintaining a regular meditation practice, and it assumes that you will first take time to self-reflect. This practice is especially useful when you want to deepen the relationship, for example, with loved ones or promising allies. It is also helpful in work situations or when you want to build bridges within and across race.

This practice is not dependent on how others respond, nor is it dependent on a positive outcome. Rather, it focuses on what you can do to speak authentically without extraneous inner distress. With practice, it cultivates stability and confidence, which supports well-being in individual interactions and well-being within communities.

You begin by sorting out your discomfort and distress. Once that is done, the remainder of the practice is used to clear the air, maintain easeful connection, and ensure an atmosphere of well-being. It is not necessary to follow the practice in order, nor is it necessary to complete the entire practice in one sitting. Consider this practice as a compass that supports more intentional and authentic communications.

To cultivate a culture of care, you must be willing to enter into mindful relationship, to engage others with wise care. This includes speaking of your concerns in a timely manner or as soon as you feel steady and clear.

General Guidelines for Talking about What Disturbs You

Enjoy your problems.

SHUNRYŪ SUZUKI

The reality is that healing happens between people.
The wound in me evokes the healer in you,
and the wound in you evokes the healer in me,
and then as the two healers, we collaborate.

RACHEL NAOMI REMEN,
author and alternative medicine practitioner

Use this tool as a framework, not as perfection. Know that words have limits and that whatever you are expecting from this conversation won't fully manifest. Some questions don't go away and won't be answered in one conversation—or ever. With practice, you will override emotional reactivity and, as Dan Siegel explained, strengthen the executive functioning of the middle prefrontal context of the brain. You will discover that you can disagree without ill will or hatred and that you can be different without someone or something being wrong. Over time, this practice becomes a habit of healing habits of harm.

Check Your Inner Experience

Reflect on these questions prior to talking about what disturbs you:

- Given this disturbance, what old traumas or wounds have been activated? Acknowledge and take care of them. You don't have to be trauma-free before you have a difficult conversation, but you do want to enter with clarity and stability.

- How is your view about the conflict influenced by your racial group identity? For example, is your upset inflamed by your dominant or subordinated group membership?

- Clarify your voice. Is your grievance addressing the individual, group, or institutional level?

- What characteristics about this person or situation can you acknowledge as good or neutral? Can you see aspects of yourself, past or present, in this person or situation?

- What thoughts, emotions, or beliefs are you convinced of or do you overly identify with?

- Are you taking this disturbance personally? Is this absolutely true?

- Do you believe this situation has always been or will always be this way? Is that absolutely true?

- Do you believe this situation should be other than it actually is right now? Can it be anything other than it actually is in this moment?

- Do you feel clear and stable enough to confront this disturbance without causing harm to others or yourself?

- What is your intention in confronting this disturbance? What outcome do you hope for? Do you want to be right, to better understand, to bridge separation, to reach agreement, and so on? Be clear about your intention without being attached to the outcome.

- Are you open to learning?

These reflections are meant to support you in staying centered and in your integrity. Be honest with yourself and find that thin line between talking and avoiding or "bypassing" what is difficult to talk about.

Once you have completed the reflections, clarify one concern that you want to address. If you have multiple concerns, pick the one that is most important. Next, initiate contact with the person you want to speak to and arrange a time to talk for fifteen minutes as a start. Keeping the time short will help you focus and keep you from overwhelming your nervous system. When you take on one issue at a time, in small doses, you can experience incremental relief, which builds inner confidence and stability. Prior to meeting, center yourself by taking three deep breaths. It is useful to remind yourself that nothing is personal, permanent, or perfect, to center your thoughts and soften the edges around the tension in your body. To sustain inner stability and presence, keep 50 percent of your awareness on your body and breath throughout the conversation. When you meet, sit face to face, if possible, where you can make gentle eye contact and observe body posture and subtle shifts. You may want to request that the person not interrupt for the first several moments. Use a tone, pace, and pitch of sincere kindness and curiosity, and remind yourself of your deepest intention.

1. AFFIRM WHAT'S GOOD AND WHAT'S SHARED

When we must discuss a difficult concern, the other person may often be afraid that their goodness will go unseen or suddenly have no value, and they will be shamed, dismissed, or made to feel completely wrong. When we start by stating what is good about the person and what is shared, we begin in humility. The ears open and the heart softens, and we instantly become more human. We feel safer to come out of hiding. If we look closely, there is always something we can genuinely appreciate in another person, and this is a great way to begin. You can make a simple statement like:

- Thank you for being willing to talk. Our friendship is important to me.

- I often find myself in agreement with you when . . . (be specific).

- I recognize how much you care about . . . (be specific).

Then state your concern clearly and briefly. Be specific about the observable behaviors you are concerned with and your feelings about them. Avoid extraneous preamble and pleasantries. Use "I" statements and avoid interpretations and statements beginning with "you," "why," "you always," "how could you," and other accusations. If you have interpretations or beliefs about what happened, own them as your own. Keep in mind that your grievance is not the sum total of the other person's character or experience. It is best if there is no hate or threat voiced in your concern: "If this doesn't stop, I'm out of here!" Or "You need to decide now!" While such statements may be tempting, this kind of charge tends to drive a wedge in the relationship. Here are some examples of stated concerns:

- It bothers me when you . . .

- I felt hurt when you . . .

- I disagree with the way you handled . . .
  for these reasons . . .

- I want both of us to feel safe, but I don't feel
  safe when . . .

2. OWN UP TO HUMANIZE THE EXCHANGE

There are very few conflicts where responsibility solely rests on one person. Why? Because you are there, affected by it! Of course, there are exceptions to this rule—for example, when a subordinated group member is confronting a dominant group member, "owning up" may further the subordination dynamic. Therefore, it is important to notice how you feel and whether there is enough presence, understanding, and respect before opening and being completely vulnerable. This step can also come later in the conversation.

When you can genuinely own up to how you have participated in the problem, it often will harmonize and neutralize what might otherwise feel like an attack. It says, "We're in this together! Take your time and give this some thought." This is at the heart of conflict and often your well-being. Some examples of how to open up:

- I know it didn't help that I was sarcastic and cynical.

- I realize that I got scared, felt caged, and then blamed you.

- I know I have a lot to learn about . . . (be specific). Please bear with me.

- You were right to point that out . . . (be specific).

- I realize my anger is older than the conflict we are having, and I'm working on it.

- I apologize for shutting down and becoming silently resentful.

- It's difficult for me to explain myself, and I have avoided talking about this, which hasn't helped.

3. SEEK UNDERSTANDING

Seeking understanding interrupts projections and cultivates empathy. You seek understanding by asking questions—one at a time—and then being quiet. When seeking understanding, slow down, check in, and breathe, as this supports stability and presence. Avoid interrupting when the other person is speaking.

Be open to softening your ego, discovering something new, and learning of your impact. Listen spaciously with your entire body, not just your ears, and relax in the quiet spaces in between what is being said. Know that people have different ways of expressing their feelings, which is particularly true when engaging across racial differences and cultures. Following are some examples of questions to ask:

- Would you tell me what you heard me saying?

- What's your understanding of what happened?
  How were you impacted?

- How did you see me contributing to this problem?

- What are we both not seeing? What do we agree on?

4. MAKE A CLEAR REQUEST

Once there is more understanding, you may have a request of the person—something that would make things work better for you and all concerned. It is wholesome to consider what others need and what you can genuinely give. Requests should be clear, respectful, and actionable and should move the relationship in the direction of respect and genuine kinship. Review Step 1: Affirm What's Good and What's Shared to clarify the outcome you seek. When making a request, it is important to be invested in the outcome but not attached to it. Make sure requests and agreements are distinct, and notice the impact your request is having on the person you are speaking to. If agreements are made, restate them for clarity, as in the following examples.

- I'd like you to point out when white people dominate the conversation and invite other voices in.

- It would be helpful if you did not assume that my experience as a person of color is the same as yours.

- I would feel safer if . . .

- Can we return to this conversation when we both feel calmer? (If agreeable, set a specific time.)

- Is my request agreeable to you?

Boundaries and agreements are important to maintain. If you feel you are making healthy progress, you can continue the discussion, but make this a clear request: "I know I requested fifteen minutes and our time is up. Is it okay if we continue?"

If you feel stuck, arrange more time later in the day or week. Setting a specific time affirms the importance of the concern and minimizes anxiety or unspoken feelings of shame, resentment, or fear. It also allows you the space to begin again and to reestablish safety in the relationship.

5. EXTEND APPRECIATION

Extending appreciation is an act of peace. It provides a graceful context to the tension often inherent in difficult conversations. It marks a finite period in the progress of the relationship and affirms that the troubling behavior is not the sum total of the person you are addressing. When you extend appreciation, you are acknowledging and appreciating goodness and your differences, and it sets a tone that says, "We can learn together." In this step, sincerely thank the other person for talking to you about your concern.

- Thank you. I appreciate that we could work this out.

- I appreciate your sincerity and care. This time means a lot to me.

- This was not easy, but we hung in together. I appreciate how you . . .

- We gave this our best shot, and I'm committed to working this out.

6. SELF-REFLECT

Talking about what disturbs you takes courage and is a leap of faith. You enter these conversations hopeful and with good intention. After taking such a risk, it is useful to reflect on the experience in your sitting practice. You might begin by reflecting on the questions outlined in Step 1 and noticing how your heart, mind, and body feel now. It is not about a happy ending, although that often happens. Rather, to reflect on yourself is to learn about yourself and your impact on others and to bring your deepest intentions into harmony with your actions. Self-reflection is often sobering and humbling.

If the discussion did not end satisfactorily, take some time to reexamine and refine your intention. For example, you may have aimed for peace in the first conversation, but clarity is the most you could achieve. Or you may have done everything possible without reaching a satisfactory outcome, and it may now be appropriate to let go and nurture any disappointment you feel by appreciating yourself for trying and offering gratitude for your fragility and resilience. You might also consider the conversation a mini-series instead of a one-time event; begin again when and if it feels right. If the conversation was satisfying, reflect on how good it feels to have clarity, reach agreements, or connect more honestly.

Concluding Thoughts:
Calling Out, Inviting In

Talking about what disturbs us is a mindfulness practice that matures over time. Regardless of your race, no one likes being called out. It does not matter how thoughtful or thoughtless the message is delivered; no one likes hearing or having the impact of their behavior pointed out to them. We feel vulnerable and over-exposed. Our delusion of being perfect or acceptable is shattered. The ego goes into distress and defense. Fundamentally, we feel shamed when the impact of our behavior is called out. In fact, there is shame all around. The person that must confront our behavior is often also shamed from being impacted by our behavior, and because they must confront it. We don't see shame; rather, we experience a twinge of anger because it is not always easy to separate the ways we have been harmfully affected.

Clearly, this is tender territory requiring sensitivity. For those being called out, it is important that you stay open to learning, to acknowledging that ego bruising is often necessary to wake up and transform habits of harm, and to being humbled by the bravery of those confronting you in an attempt to foster a more honest exchange. For those calling out, be willing to recognize the fragility of being human, which includes ignorance, innocence, and ill will, and invite the person into learning rather than just calling them into humiliation.

Even with our best efforts, it can be messy. Primarily, we want to keep our fingers on the pulse of good intention, do our best, and never give up on the human spirit. Talking about what disturbs you is not a practice of perfection but a practice of humility that keeps us learning about what it means to be human. This practice is not meant to be linear; rather, it is an intuitive compass for navigating the terrain of racial distress. When we can offer the right questions and allow space, others, as well as ourselves, can come out of hiding into more light. We discover together what it means to be human.

15

What White People Can Do with Privilege

Dear White People: No one is asking you to apologize for your ancestors. We are asking you to dismantle the system of oppression they built that you maintain and benefit from.

MICHAEL ERIC DYSON, author and radio host

n this chapter, I am speaking specifically to white people in an attempt to deepen the inquiry into whiteness and wise action. As you develop more racial literacy through the teachings in this book and in your own lives, there are a few additional thoughts to consider as white individuals, as white groups, and as white leaders within organizations and institutions.

Own Whiteness

I've already explained the importance of white people owning their racial group identity and exploring what that means through white racial affinity groups. As mentioned, you don't need to recruit POC to wake up to whiteness; you just need each other, at least initially.

In examining the racial inheritance of white group identity, you might ask, "What happened to the historical or inherited trauma that goes hand in hand with hating another race? What was passed on to us? How does it live today? How did we survive? How is it that we have managed to be okay or considered superior as a race?"

The racial crime is in disowning whiteness while still benefiting from whiteness. Memory is the most challenging part of racial healing. Coming together as white people and tenderly examining this thing called whiteness that other races seem to know about is a crucial link in racial healing and harmony.

An experience I had sticks with me. An older white male meditator called to thank me after hearing one of my talks on being mindful of race. He spoke of his poor upbringing in the South, where his family and the entirety of his community openly hated blacks. He described how he couldn't wait to leave home, which he did in his early twenties, never to return. He shared his confusion growing up because the blacks he saw were as poor as he was, but his family and community felt superior. I asked, "Given your mindfulness practice and your growing racial awareness, how would it be for you to go back home and talk to your family about how their racial hatred impacted your life?" Immediately he replied, "Oh, no. I could never do that! They would never listen." After a pause, I repeated, "How would it be for *you*?"

Why is "not going there" the habitual choice for many whites? Whites must ask themselves, "Is it true that other whites won't listen, or is it that I want to avoid the subject because of the discomfort that I would experience in broaching the subject? Or am I afraid of being disliked or not being agreed with?"

This returning to the scene of the crime, so to speak, is the work of whiteness, and to cringe at the thought of returning is privilege at play. To leave the scene of the crime and not return, to not confront the roots of whiteness within your family and discuss its impact on you individually, is a choice whites can and do make as individuals. However, this choice leaves the weight of white ignorance and resistance on the shoulders of POC.

One white woman leader I coached was anxious about being correct in framing how to give credit to a Korean artist she was introducing at a conference. I took this as an opportunity to invite her to explore why this framing was producing such anxiety for her. I invited her to do an experiment over the next few weeks: when introducing or referencing a white person, she was to refer to them and herself as white. I wanted her to have the chance to think about herself as a white woman with privileges, in that whiteness rarely has to be named. Even if she chose not to take this challenge, I asked her to simply notice how it feels to consider doing so, how it feels to be a person of color—a card-carrying member of a white racial group.

Awkward and reluctant, she took the challenge. Humbly, she reported that it was a very useful experiment that made her much more aware of her blindness and the privilege of whiteness, not to mention touching into her own fear of claiming whiteness. As we further explored her fear of claiming whiteness, she shared that it had to do with belonging and safety. I asked, "Belonging to what, exactly?" After an awkward pause, she replied, "I'm not sure, but the question feels alarmingly important to ponder." This discomfort—this naming, this coming out, this exposure to light—is the territory that whites, especially, must investigate as racial beings.

In my Mindful of Race training program, I often put same-race people in groups to explore various aspects of their racial group identity. Commonly, when white people gather in a group to talk about race, they feel puzzled and confused about what they should talk about. They often say that they feel irritated and awkward, unable to have a conversation about race unless POC are present. They feel suspicious and set up being in a group of whites.

On one such occasion, white men and women were put in a small group, and the interactions quickly became strained.

A white woman asked a white man to talk about what it was like being a white male. He instantly became outraged, while the other whites in the group remained silent. In the group processing that followed, the white male shared that he felt that he had been disrespected, but he couldn't explain why. Others in the group felt like they were witnessing cruelty, but they felt small and frozen and didn't feel safe enough to intervene. The white woman was fuming in silent rage from being silenced by the white male and unsupported by others in the group.

After inviting them to feel into their present experience (recognize and allow), I asked them to consider if an implicit group code had been violated as it relates to race and gender—that is, that white women were never to tell white men to examine themselves in public, especially in matters of race. In this case, the white male was exercising his dominant privilege as white and male. Through his actions, the white woman was put in her place—gender subordination—and those who witnessed colluded in silence.

Many white women are outraged over gender oppression, especially from white men. When whites of mixed genders are challenged to talk about race, gender conflicts often will trump racial inquiry. The discussion heatedly shifts from race to gender.

When white women insist on talking about race, they are often referred to as angry and strident. White men who broach racial ignorance and injury share that they are often bullied, ignored, or dismissed. These are examples of losing membership or being subordinated in an unacknowledged dominant racial group identity.

Understandably, white people struggle as they wake up to whiteness, and for some, their growing awareness breeds a low tolerance for white ignorance. One white woman I coach shared, "It's hard being around other whites because I don't feel enough humility among us. Being white means you are good at being right, and this gets in the way of our humility."

Humility is an experience we open to when we are willing to take risks. For example, a white person talking to whites about race is an uncomfortable choice but a necessary one. A white male senior teacher of a large, predominantly white Buddhist community invited me to speak to his group, who were distressed over the increasing number of killings by police of unarmed black people. I asked him to say more about how people were feeling and what he felt I could do to help. He said the white people in his community were outraged and frightened; they felt helpless and ashamed. He thought I could help because I had more expertise in talking about these issues.

After a flash of flattery, I asked him to close his eyes. I guided him in a meditation to first feel into the outrage, fear, helplessness, and shame of being white. I then invited him to sense what he needed as a white male—what would bring a sense of grounded care while staying present to the distress. We paused here for a few breaths. I next invited him to envision himself talking to his white group about racial distress and asked him what he saw himself offering them.

He shared that he saw himself sharing how hurt and helpless he felt over the killings and that as a white man he felt he should be able to do something but didn't know what to do. He said he would offer a guided meditation on compassion and follow that by inviting them to speak in small groups about their fears and concerns. After hearing of his plan and declining his invitation, I reassured him that he had everything he needed. I encouraged him to talk to his community about whiteness—to expand from individual despair to collective inquiry of cause and effect and to feel into their kinship with white police officers. For example, "Who are we as white people together? How do we become more racially literate about whiteness? What can we do to ensure racial harmony among ourselves?"

White people may never have as much experience as POC in talking about racial distress and racism, but they must start, especially if they are in leadership positions. Whites can use their privilege to model what it's like to wake up to being white. I coach a number of white meditation teachers who are interested in becoming more racially aware of themselves and their impact as teachers. In their talks, many reference political issues of immigrants, Jews, Mexicans, Asians, blacks, Muslims, and American Indians. They may even speak of the need to understand other races. However, rarely is white supremacy mentioned, nor do they refer to themselves as white people. It's as if they were a nice clean white plate untouched by the gravy. Referencing other individuals and races that struggle and are triumphant is important, but even more important is white people learning about white history and its impact on other races.

There is an edgy side to learning about white history, and it has to do with consciousness. For example, when white people become aware of themselves as white, they may prefer being associated with its supremacy. The latest mutation of the white supremacist movement as represented by members of the alt-right, for example, is that their consciousness leads not to humility or a willingness to respect other races but rather to fear: a sense that the white race is in danger of being polluted by contact with people of other races and that the whites will lose control of this country. This fear was threatened by the previous administration being headed by an African American president. When white nationalists are the only whites talking about white group identity, it can force other whites to avoid claiming whiteness out of a fear of association. What is needed are more conscious white people to talk about themselves as a racial group.

If you are a white person becoming mindful of race, you have stories to tell about what it's like waking up to whiteness and its impact on other races, including white struggles and contributions to humanity. When you tell such stories, you demonstrate a way for other whites to talk about race, and that holds the promise of shifting the social narrative from dominance to synergy. As a white leader, share your journey of waking up to whiteness and learn about and reference other whites who model guidance through their own example.

In the absence of knowing and talking about whiteness, white individuals and white groups will appropriate cultures of color in both gross and subtle ways. Cultural appropriation is when the dominant culture takes, borrows, or exploits, for personal gain, comfort, or pleasure, the cultural expressions, experiences, and possessions of another group deemed subordinated. For example, whites violently and systematically stole sacred land from American Indians, claimed it as their own, distorted the history of American Indians, forced them to sign treaties, and then manipulated those treaties for capital gain. Cultural appropriation includes the taking of symbols, traditions, land, emotions, spiritual ceremonies, artifacts, and energy.

Cultural appropriation can also be subtle and day-to-day. A white man in the Mindful of Race training shared that he facilitates a support group of predominantly black men in the prison system, mainly because he felt more alive when he heard their stories—"I needed my weekly fix!" When I asked him to tell me his story or to tell me about white people near and dear to him who have found a way out of suffering, he had no response, yet I doubt that he had no stories.

I don't want to dismiss the goodwill of his service in the prison system, but I do want to point to the tendency some whites have of feeding on the energy of black lives and other POC, often without awareness, transparency, or consent. For many POC, cultural appropriation, once recognized, is experienced as a dominant culture getting away with a soul crime. Nonconsent is the aggravated assault when such thievery is at play.

It's important for white people to know that whiteness has impact and that this impact is not separate from them. Setting the intention to pause, notice impact (as an individual and group member), and question habitual impulses that breed entitlement is a critical practice. In her book, *Time to Stand Up: An Engaged Buddhist Manifesto for Our Earth*, Thanissara, a white woman and social activist, shared a pointed story of such a pause when she realized the nuances of internalized privilege:

> As I entered the supermarket, I walked toward the metal baskets that were piled on top of each other. An elderly Zulu man was struggling to pull out the top basket. The moment it released, I reached out to take it assuming he was a worker, when actually he was there to shop. At that moment, my liberal, progressive identity dissolved into shock as I realized I had internalized the racist Apartheid system of South Africa that saw black people as workers and white people as their boss. The great wave of shame ultimately didn't help. What's more important to see is how a system, that I hadn't actually been born into or raised in, could so quickly and unconsciously be internalized. That I was party to an insidious systemic racism that privileged me as a white person, even though this man was an elder and I was a guest in his country. My lack of awareness made me culpable in the terrible injustice of racism, while at the same time the sharp increase of awareness catalyzed by this seemingly small incident left me flooded with complexity.

Waking up to our habits of harm is not always a warm and fuzzy experience. In fact, it can feel quite agonizing, and it comes with moral responsibility. For this reason, most people with privilege don't bother to go down this route—why bother? Therefore, for those of you reading this book and committing yourselves to so dare, it is important to practice patience and self-compassion. The practice of transforming racism from the inside out builds humility.

Talk to Children about Whiteness

Children feel and fear more than they understand or can articulate about race. For example, in an all-white corporate team-building session, Elizabeth shared that there was never a mention of race in her household growing up. Her family was proud, and there was a sense of superiority, but it wasn't associated with race. Jessie, another member, spoke of growing up hearing verbal outrage toward other races from the adults in his family. He said he often felt anxious and tense, but he knew not to talk about it.

What happens in a family, whether conscious or not, still lives in a family—the good, the bad, and the ugly. We all play a part in patterns of racial harm—the constellations—until we can acknowledge and transform them. A precious way to talk to our children about race is through personal storytelling. Storytelling can be an act of love—a way to deepen connections, heal, and experience care. What insights or personal stories might you tell your children about whiteness so they are supported in understanding, celebrating, and healing their history?

While on a meditation retreat, I was woken up by a dream early one morning, and the following story made its way to paper. I call it "The Untold," and it is a story white people might consider telling to their children or adapting to their experience:

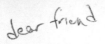
dear friend

My child, I'd like to tell you, from my lips, the truth about our racial history—about whiteness and about being a member of the white tribe. Years ago, our ancestors did a horrific deed against the human race. They owned black people as slaves and treated them with utter disrespect. Beatings, rape, torture, lynching, ongoing terror; we sold their children to the highest bidders and owned them as possessions. And we relied on them to grow our food and take care of our children—your ancestors. Yes, our people did this—white people. Not only did we do this to blacks; we also did hateful things to people who we felt were substandard, like American Indians, Mexicans, Jews, Japanese, Chinese, and poorer people than we were.

It's true that the greatness of this country, to a large extent, is due to the slave labor of blacks, and we owe them a huge debt. We have, as a white race, disenfranchised them and systematically organized to keep them from participating in and benefiting from the wealthiest country in the world. Our success, however big or small, and the many privileges we enjoy as a family are rooted in this stained and denied history. Even to this day, our people benefit from the institutional practices that intentionally and systematically oppress black and other dark bodies. Many poor white people feel that they are better than black people—even better than the first black president of the United States.

Being ashamed about this is not as helpful as understanding that we have a lot of work to do to begin to respect blacks and dark lives, to release and share the wealth and privileges we have for all they have given to us as white people.

Blacks and other POC are rightfully angry toward us because of the centuries of hatred and disrespect we have shown them. We have continued as a collective to build prisons to hide and erase them, instead of facing the years of hatred toward them and shame toward ourselves that have resulted in destroyed hearts, minds, and communities. Most important, we have died inside as a result of making hatred normal as a race. We have become numb, dismembered, crude, and unloving toward our own race, because we cannot access the depth of love as a collective with such a stained and unfinished history of disrespect and hatred toward other humans.

What this means to you and me is that we must wake up to this history and own that we walk with great ease in this country on their still sore backs—backs we whipped into submission. What we witness today in the black collective expression is the result of generations of blacks who have witnessed their parents and grandparents killed, lynched, raped by our men, and hated and disrespected by us. They were helpless against it—we made sure of that.

You need to understand, my child, that while we have other fears, we tend to walk without racial fear, and they don't. This world is not safe for them and other people like them—dark people—and it is because of our history, our whiteness. To this day we have better schools and access, and we still are the central race in all aspects of respectable society, work, and leadership. Black communities are largely poor, and their schools are disenfranchised because we have kept them at a disadvantage. Many of them are considered criminals, even though they are not doing anything more than we do in our communities. Yet they are imprisoned and used again as slave labor.

Many whites want to maintain white supremacy, and there continues to be white nationalist rallies and terror attacks on other races near and far, currently emboldened by senior members of the White House.

We have done horrible things as a white race, unspeakable things, yet we have not spoken or been honest with each other or ourselves as a white race. While you and I may not have done these things personally, this is our history and our inheritance.

Our challenge is to do everything humanly possible to recognize and interrupt any act of disrespect and unearned privilege and to use our voices, our bodies, and our hearts to make this wrong right. We need this in order to be free. This does not mean kissing up to blacks or anyone else, although it may seem that way. Rather it means a willingness to face into the pain they carry because we've been so cavalier, numb, and blind to the role we have played in the past and present horrors of their lives.

Our job now and for a long time is to own up to it, apologize, and recognize that their expressed pain is not directed to you or me as an individual but to us as a white race and as the institutional power that continues to oppress them, often through our ignorance, greed, comfort, righteousness, and indifference.

I tell you this because you may well receive much disdain from black people. When they see you, they are also seeing our unclaimed and terrorizing history; they see you as someone who, like our forefathers, hated them, and they see our ignorance, the way we casually delight in a disowned and forgotten history—a history where we considered them as less than human, as possessions, as chattel. This history wasn't that long ago. They are and should be hurt and angry by our utter neglect and generational hatred.

There is much to be done. There is no time for guilt and shame. We must forgive ourselves and correct this wrong. We must become advocates for all of humanity, especially black and dark-skinned bodies. Enough said for now, but we will speak of this again and again and again.

As a white person, what comes up for you as you consider telling your child—or any white person—such a story? If you are feeling uneasy or queasy or have an aversion to verbalizing such a story, you might ask yourself why. What beliefs or emotions get in the way? If "The Untold" feels too far-fetched, what stories feel closer to you? Consider personalizing this exercise so that it reflects the truth of your individual experience as a racial being and your history as a racial group. Not being willing to speak freely about such racial truths, in your own words, is how white supremacy is upheld and privilege is maintained.

Dismantle Structural Racism

Fundamental to being human is our fear of exclusion and our desire for inclusion. We all want to belong. Once we feel we belong, we turn our attention to the span of control we have to influence our own destiny. Influencing and controlling our destiny is a process bound to be fraught with interpersonal and social conflicts, especially among races. Conflict, if we can stay with it and learn from it, can often deepen human connection. When we feel the satisfaction of being included and have learned from conflict, we can take more risks and be more intimate and transparent with each other. However, as humans, we have not been successful at resolving racial conflict in ways that support openness and transparency and that ensure well-being for all races.

White supremacy within institutions has historically controlled not only the power to include and exclude but also the power to control the destiny and well-being of other races. For example, in every direction of our day-to-day lives, whether in jobs, schools, leadership, government, legal and law enforcement, medical fields, or the media, whiteness is portrayed as the standard of beauty and prosperity, with an occasional sprinkling of color. POC, by and large, have been required to advocate for inclusion and to insist on controlling the welfare of their own lives. This deep-grooved pattern is held in place through structural racism, which is the ideology of whiteness as expressed in policies, practices, strategies, and standard ways of operating. Structural racism maintains white supremacy and white power. Structural racism is often rooted in greed—gain that is often at the expense of an "other." Greed, often disguised as capitalism, is fundamental to Western civilization.

Although structural racism is embedded in leadership practices, it is often invisible to white leaders and, if pointed out, often dismissed. As I have stressed throughout this book, structural racism is invisible and dismissed because white people have not vetted whiteness and its impact. As a result, white leaders, by default, through the exercise of their power, can only reflect the racial consciousness they carry as individuals. This racial power and unconsciousness predictably breed an institutional climate of racism, even if this was not a conscious intent. Such norms promote conflict and feelings of exclusion among POC and negatively affect belonging and harmony. But the reverse is also true. If the dominant group is willing to be aware of its white group identity, dominance, and impact, such awareness begins to influence the norm of organizational and social life in more equitable and inclusive ways.

Power is not inherently abusive. Whites with institutional power and racial consciousness can become morally responsible by using their power for good, if they are willing to be condemned by those who resent their attempts at greater equity. If this sounds like a high risk, consider that this is precisely the daily experience of many POC and poor whites inside and outside of white institutions. With self-awareness and a vision that extends beyond self-interest and organizational gain, white leaders can become more curious about the human systems in organizational and institutional life—the structures of both harm and harmony. They can examine, with other leaders, the policies and practices, rewards and punishments that block equity and inclusion.

For example, white leaders might examine the attitudes behind profit and loss by asking, "How much profit is enough? Who is harmed in our gain?" They might reimagine how and where financial resources are spent and who or what is exploited. They might seek diverse points of view and experiment with different power structures. They might ask, "How do we create more balance and fairness? Whose voices do we listen to most? What voices are habitually left out?" They might also examine policies on hiring quotas and promotion and performance practices by asking, "What do we reward and punish? What qualities do we seek, and who defines them? Are our leaders trained in racial awareness and literacy and held accountable through performance measures? What are the consequences of poor performance and misconduct?"

A culture change is required to ensure inclusion and belonging, and that culture change requires skill, willingness, and time for process, not just the completion of tasks. To have diversity on the team without a process for team reflection and cultural learning is tokenism. Tokenism is a form of window dressing in which whites appoint POC and make assumptions about who people are and what is important to them. Commonly, whites blindly assume that whoever is hired or joins their team is happy to be there, wants to be like them, and will go with the flow—but they are wrong. Most POC are not trying to be white; they are trying to be themselves, use their own minds, and have what they bring be recognized and valued. The very presence of POC signifies the need for change and invites a reexamination of who we are together inside social systems that were not originally designed with them in mind.

Lead Culture Change Initiatives within Organizations

Many white leaders inside organizations have the power to influence racial inclusion and equity by aligning policies and practices, educating leaders to manage culture change, and holding leaders accountable for their actions and impact.

It is important to understand that culture change is not the same as diversity or racial awareness training programs. Training is a strategy that supports culture change, but it cannot be the only intervention. To address culture change inside institutions, white leaders must understand that often the *culture* of whiteness is being examined and asked to *change*—that is, to align in ways that support the espoused institutional values of inclusion and equity. This usually sounds fine until people are impacted, feel exposed, or are inconvenienced by the time required and assessments necessary to understand how the current culture habitually functions.

Even when white leaders begin a culture change initiative with good intentions, they must be reminded again and again that culture change is the examination and transformation of values, beliefs, policies, structures, and rewards. In such a process, how individuals and the institution as an entity relate to change is activated, as is the edginess stimulated when racial biases and structural racism are being examined. Individual beliefs and organizational structures and systems that keep the organization functioning are often the same apparatus that works against culture change. The very nature of true culture change is to bring existing habits of harm to light so they can be addressed more consciously and equitably.

It is important to examine the motivation behind initiating culture change. For example, some leaders may have gotten excited about a training they attended or a book they read. Or they may have been encouraged by a friend who had success with a program; they immediately want to bring these ideas into the organization, only to be met with resistance. In such instances, the "culture" has not been prepared for the training, and the systems have not been prepared to support and reinforce the learning. This is *training*, not culture change, and such a tactic often results in people going through the motions of attending training and then returning to work as usual. There is no accountability.

Sometimes white leaders create a diversity policy, new guidelines, or training program for the entire team in order to avoid giving direct feedback to or to pacify a grievance of a person of color. Another avoidance tactic is when white leaders want to support a person of color they are challenged with by making coaching available, often by a POC coach. This strategy is often independent of a white leader's understanding of the cultural context of whiteness within which the person of color is functioning. In other words, in this thought process, it is the person of color who needs help, not the system—albeit both may be true.

Whatever the reason, the belief by most white leaders who are in a position to initiate a movement of racial awareness is that, because they have bought into the idea and have good intentions, others will be just as happy, and the initiative will be smooth sailing with minimal disruption. Of course, this is often not the case.

To address racism inside institutions is to begin a journey of transforming the culture of whiteness, and to transform the culture of whiteness requires an examination and realignment of human structures—a change in the way work and relationships happen. Such an initiative involves changing hearts and shifting power. There is nothing simple about it; it's messy, even on a good day. Leaders who have undertaken racial awareness initiatives, only to feel discouraged, have not failed. Rather, they have experienced a kink in a long chain of learning. Such initiatives require professional support and a commitment to process more than to the sureness of a goal.

If you are considering starting a racial awareness and culture change initiative, or if you have began such an initiative and want fortification, first form a white leaders RAG following the guidelines in chapter 13. Consider this group a permanent structure and priority that supports waking up to whiteness and its impact on culture change. Second, be sure that senior leaders are leading culture change initiatives and invest in a partnership with skilled consultants external to the organization who specialize in culture change, not just in training programs.

It is important to have a broad base of internal input for culture change, but beware: many people in the organization who have passion, opinions, and history will be appropriately biased and will likely lack the skills required to understand the systemic and political intricacies of such a change. Even more complicated is when a white leader tags a POC inside the organization as a primary source of input. Such an informal gesture blurs the business relationship, leads to more work for the POC, and can become politically awkward. For example, pointing out whiteness and power dynamics carries a high risk for the person of color and can feel personal for the white leader. Such a relationship can also be viewed as favoritism by other POC and as tokenism by whites. The person of color may also become the target of failure or be pigeonholed when the waves of resistance are strong, which is to be expected with such an initiative.

Commonly, senior leaders will delegate diversity and racial initiatives to a person—often a POC—or to a committee to administer. The individual or committee generally has responsibility without power, and the white leaders of the organization are removed from engagements that support racial literacy and intimacy with change. Delegation of cultural change trivializes the initiative and the expertise, accountability, and importance required for sustained culture change. It also says to members of the organization that they don't have to take the initiative seriously.

Training programs raise awareness; accountability changes culture. To support accountability and integration, link training and culture change initiatives to performance management, organizational privileges, and leadership compensation.

Organize a Racial Human Rights Movement

I am in earnest—I will not equivocate—I will not excuse—
I will not retreat a single inch—and I will be heard.
WILLIAM LLOYD GARRISON, journalist and white abolitionist

A significant number of white individuals and groups do not want to change the power dynamics of white supremacy in this country. With the rise of the alt-right and the new white supremacy movement, led by people like Richard Spencer, who spearheaded the march in Charlottesville, Virginia, many white people feel they have been disadvantaged or dishonored by immigrant growth and an emphasis on racial equality. They fear that the white race will become extinct if drastic measures are not taken. This is an ominous development, played upon by political strategists like Steve Bannon to promote regressive racial policies.

Congress and the Tea Party rigorously demonstrated racism toward President Obama throughout his term, and white nationalists across the nation have been emboldened through the racist, misogynist, and xenophobic ideology of President Trump's agenda to Make America Great Again, a slogan interpreted by many as to Make America *White* Again.

At the time of this writing, a violent outbreak of racial hatred erupted in Charlottesville, Virginia, a state, like many, that is no stranger to racism or race war. A month after a Ku Klux Klan rally primed the pump in the city, torch-bearing white nationalists protested near the Thomas Jefferson statue on the grounds of the University of Virginia, chanting, "You will not replace us" and "Jews will not replace us." A brawl ensued with counterprotestors. The next day, the Unite the Right rally, which included the alt-right, neo-Nazis, Confederate loyalists, and militia, demonstrated in the streets, protesting the removal of a statue of Robert E. Lee, commander of the Confederate Army of Northern Virginia during the US Civil War. In a park formerly named Lee Park but recently renamed Emancipation Park by the local city council, protesters carried swastika flags, Confederate battle flags, anti-Muslim and anti-Semitic banners, and Trump/Pence signs.

Counterprotesters attended in opposition to white supremacy, representing a wide range of ideologies and tactics—some peaceful and others more aggressive. Some of the organizations included Black Lives Matter, National Council of Churches, Charlottesville Clergy Collective, Anti-Racist Action, Antifa, and the Democratic Socialists of America. Jewish, Muslim, Christian, and Buddhist faiths united and were engaged in resistance, educational, and mindfulness strategies. Guest celebrities offered talks and trainings, and businesses offered space for refuge.

The march became violent. Dozens were injured from physical shoves and fights. A white man crashed his car into a crowd, killing a thirty-two-year-old white woman and injuring nineteen protesters. Two police officers died in a helicopter crash while supervising the grounds. The city was declared a state of emergency.

The president of the United States offered an inadequate response when he condoned the white nationalists, stating that everyone shared responsibility for the violence. The president's pardoning of the hateful intent of the white nationalists riveted the nation and said to its people that it is acceptable to publically exhibit racial prejudice and to fight to regain and maintain racial dominance. Several business leaders and state officials resigned and withdrew support because of the president's message, and the mayor of Charlottesville told the hate groups, "Go home. You have no place here. You are not patriots." But where, exactly, is home?

At a glance, many of the people the media captured protesting and counterprotesting in Charlottesville—and in the many cities that protested across the country following the Charlottesville eruption—were white people. The white people representing hate groups are family; they belong to us. There is no "go home" other than "returning to us," which is to say returning home to white people who are waking up to whiteness.

Hatred toward other races is learned behavior. When whites hold on to the sharp edges of hate, the heart arteries are clogged. It's divisive, and it limits intimacy among white people. It feeds the misconception of superiority, and it inhibits social solidarity. When there is a racial other, righteousness, fear, and comfort can mask such anguish and sorrow. The need here, first and foremost, is for whites who are becoming mindful of race to become interested in this shadowed reflection of whiteness and to both challenge it and support its healing.

There is more that white people can do with white privilege. What if confronting racism were no longer the sole work of POC? Instead, what if white people, on a large scale, galvanized resources to organize and lead a human rights movement focused on dismantling white supremacy inside institutions, communities, and families? What if white people made it their business to eliminate all racial barriers to POC—enforcement, compliance, warehousing, imprisoning, deportation, bombing, building walls of exclusion, placing limits on jobs and health care, and other blocks to a thriving livelihood?

What if whites used their collective power to reimagine security, policing, and punishment in this country and throughout the world? What if masses of white people asked other white people questions like, "Why are there so many POC and poor people in prison? Are they all bad people? Why did they do what they did? What was it rooted in—mental or physical abilities, poverty, or homelessness? What policies and practices ensure such injury? In what ways do we as whites exploit this situation? How do we make things worse through our drive for gain or indifference? In what ways do we disadvantage society as white people? What response would support a structure of healing and rejuvenation? What would it be like if policies, practices, and laws came into alliance with such human rights care?"

A white male senior executive in a Fortune 500 corporation shared this story:

> I was so disturbed by the distress calls from Hurricane Irma that hit the Florida shores that, on an impulse, I asked a crew of colleagues and interested team players to join me in renting a few trucks and driving to Florida to help families clear out their homes. The health risks for families who did not clear out the debris was life

threatening, and many people were not receiving the immediate attention they needed.

We landed in a flooded community of mostly African American, low-income families and began the task of clearing out debris that was quickly turning into toxic mold. One elderly black woman, who happened to be a hoarder, was resisting having any of her items thrown out, arguing that she just couldn't let it go. Her home was deeply flooded and packed from floor to ceiling with what appeared to be neatly organized and compacted trash. I took the elderly woman outside and for the longest time explained to her that she would die if her home were not cleared. The woman finally paused long enough to look into my eyes; then she simply sobbed, knowing that what I was saying was true as the crew finished the clearing.

In the middle of this horrific task, I received a call from the legal department of my company saying that my venture to the hurricane-hit area was putting the company in jeopardy and that I was to return immediately. I replied, "You can send a crew down here to show me how what I am doing is at risk and then advise me on how to keep us all safe." I hung up the phone and never heard another word from them. We did what we could do in five days, then returned home. As it turned out, it wasn't an issue for my company.

This story shows one example of what white people in power can do with privilege when the heart's pull is stronger than comfort or norms. This leader was able to respond, and the "standard operating procedures" of his corporation were not uppermost in his mind. Mostly, he was willing to take a risk and use what power he had for good.

Whites must challenge each other to imagine racial well-being for all! What would it be like for whites to insist of other whites that we shift away from criminalizing and fearing color to seeing our diverse and shared nature; a shift from comparing POC to a white industry standard? What might the alternatives be? What would it be like to trust that we were truly sharing in humankind? What would it be like if there were equal energetic labor? What would it be like if no race had to be afraid and if everyone could exist with grace and dignity? What if this movement dominated all forms of media, with each day our mind being blown by the goodwill of whites to eliminate domination and create racial balance and synergy?

Imagine a global mass of conscious and determined white people leading a nonviolent movement to end racism and white supremacy and restore balance. Imagine a movement that is mobilized not because POC are insisting or because white hate groups or white dominance are resisting. It's not a movement driven from guilt, shame, or ego gain. Rather, imagine a movement of heart—a moral imperative for humankind.

Most leaders of notable racial movements have been members of subordinated racial groups who defend POC and poor people against the harm and hate of white supremacy and other subtler forms of domination. Such weight can be shared, and it can start with whites using their power and privilege for good.

In US history, there have always been white people who fought against white supremacy in favor of racial justice. Find out about the white freedom fighters that came before you. Learn about their lives. Find out what worked and what didn't. Research the individuals and groups who are doing this work today and join them.

Would you join or organize such a movement? If so, why? If not, why not? Consider a movement a good use of white privilege—a missing link in the long struggle for racial freedom for all. The work won't be completed in your lifetime, but it must begin and continue.

16

What People of Color Must Do Together

*Handling our suffering is an art. If we know how to suffer,
we suffer much less, and we're no longer afraid of being
overwhelmed by the suffering inside. Instead, we should
fear not knowing how to handle our suffering.*

THICH NHAT HANH, *The Art of Living*

I n this chapter, I am speaking to people of color, offering a
few suggestions on what we can do to support the diversity of
color we represent. As a person of color, I may use the terms
"we," "our," or POC to refer to us as a collective body of color.

I'd like to begin by acknowledging that racial ignorance,
hatred, and injustice are not new struggles. Our ancestors
faced hardships more challenging than those we face today,
and our hardships will likely not be eradicated in our lifetime.
This cold fact leaves most of the people on the planet—and the
dark body of the planet herself—in jeopardy. The harsh reality
of racial life for POC is that there are no guarantees from ignorance or harm, no safety net. Hearts will be broken, and bodies
will be harmed. But we are not victims. We are works of art.

The Japanese art form of *kintsukuroi* is translated as "golden
repair." Instead of discarding broken pottery, the pottery is
artistically mended using lacquer dusted with powdered gold,
platinum, or silver as a way of preserving and dignifying the
pottery's history. The pottery is not considered flawed once

repaired, nor is it expected to function as originally intended. Rather, it is transformed into art—an object of creativity and admiration. The opportunity that POC have when we come together is to practice "golden repair."

We might begin by examining the assumptions we have made about what the term *people of color* means to us as individuals and as members of racial groups. One common understanding of this term is that it was coined to represent racial groups who were historically oppressed by whites; racial groups who share the experience of having been systematically, generationally, and continuously marginalized and oppressed in the United States because of race and skin color. Of course, there are likely many more meanings to the term.

Next, we must inquire into how we have been impacted as individuals and as racial groups—and herein lies the diversity among us. Each racial group has its own stories about and experiences of oppression, even if they don't use the term *people of color*. There is much we can learn and offer each other when we begin to rely on our capacity to wake up, heal, and suffer well.

Attend to Internalized Oppression

It is important to discern and transform internalized oppression within the diversity of subordinated racial groups. However, this is not so simple because of the subtle and nuanced nature of such oppression. White supremacy has been an intravenous drip in our consciousness for generations; a part so integral to US history and culture that it is not in our consciousness to notice it. We, therefore, need each other to wake up to how it is expressed and to discern its impact on a culture of care.

Talking about internalized oppression can be difficult. It activates old wounds we would like to think were healed, and it can feel like oppression on top of oppression. But that should not stop us from unpacking and airing out this fundamental programing of racial harm.

There are many ways internalized oppression is lived in the body of color. One way I've noticed its expression is that when we come together to talk across race, a hierarchy of oppression can emerge. I refer to this as the racial pyramid of subordinated suffering. It has to do with an indirect combat of distress we express to ensure that everyone knows "We suffer the most." It's as if POC are proving to all who will listen, "Will the real person of color please stand?" We don't do this on purpose; rather, we are driven to be visible and to climb out of our own pain by any means necessary. And yet, in doing so, we set up a hierarchy among POC mimicking white supremacy.

For example, when African Americans speak about race, what they tend to know best is their experience as African Americans. They feel that their pain represents a high rung on the pyramid of suffering because of the historic and present-day cruelty toward African Americans in this country. Such passion is necessary to express, and it has impact. Many POC who are not African Americans have shared with me that they feel silenced and invisible in racial dialogue with African Americans—unable to voice their pain or to feel that their racial experiences are taken seriously or are as significant. They share that they feel their oppression is considered minor compared to the pains of African Americans. They admit having colluded or suppressed expression of their need in order to avoid conflict and have opted instead to focus on the greater charge against white oppression. Yet this choice reinforces for them a sense of invisibility and unworthiness. In such instances, African Americans are perceived as dominant or "privileged," occupying a higher rung on the racial pyramid of subordinated suffering, and the other POC, in turn, are further subordinated. Similarly, in my conversations with a number of American Indians over the years, they often feel that the long-standing concerns of their systemic obliteration, largely due to race, have essentially been ignored for generations and that their voices have landed on deaf ears from most races.

Most racially oppressed groups, whether openly verbal or silently pissed, feel the need to have their pain acknowledged and not subordinated, especially by other POC. It is not the intention of POC to overshadow other races, nor do we set out to compete with each other. It is that our shared oppression as POC is not intimately understood among us, nor are our energies unified.

Understandably, for a person of color, unless you have absorbed yourself in other cultures of color, what you know most intimately and feel most passionately is your own experience as a racial individual and racial group. Therefore, we must set an intention to understand the body of color beyond our racial group identity.

Part of the programing of internalized oppression is to distress each other, to believe in scarcity, and to believe we are unworthy as individuals and as a body of color. This leaves us fighting, often unknowingly, against each other to disprove this unnerving conditioning. Such fighting forces us to fixate on our own pain—and whenever we fixate, someone else is left out of view. This painful dynamic keeps us separate and distracted from recognizing and experiencing our belonging.

Such squabbling is exploited through structural racism. For example, you will seldom see more than a representative number of POC in any institution owned and run by whites. Instead, the majority of hires are still white. Hiring POC is still largely a matter of meeting quotas or appearances. POC are vetted and accepted if they are perceived by white leaders to be "a good fit," meaning manageable or nonthreatening. This privileged access is limited, and POC are then required to compete for it. Such rationing of scraps pits POC against each other. We are not consciously intending to compete with other POC. Our reactivity in the face of perceived scarcity is rooted in survival and fear and a desire to be visible.

Immigrants experience their own flavors of color privilege and subordination. In the United States, darker-skinned immigrants who are considered dominant in their country of origin find themselves subordinated in North America—lumped into a generalized category of color subordination. This experience can be shocking and puzzling. Two businessmen I worked with here in the States proudly told me, "If African Americans tried harder, they too could be successful." They felt privileged in their status as Nigerian men, yet they struggled to find their dominance accepted and affirmed in the United States. They were outraged to share that when they were stopped by white police officers, "We were treated like the average black guy."

There are many ways in which internalized oppression is experienced at the group identity level. This painful and complex dynamic results in hurt, bitterness, and separations within the color body.

Another way in which internalized racism plays itself out is in how we have been conditioned to relate to each other within our own race—that is, how we have internalized the dominant cultural belief that we are flawed and unworthy. This conditioning is often reflected in our fear and distrust of each other, in how we can be overly critical and unforgiving of each other—ourselves included. We must fight to go against this entrenched programing.

A Jewish man I coached who identifies as white was highly distressed over seeing that his adult son, whom he described as dark skinned, had been mistaken as Muslim and verbally attacked on his way home. He didn't know what he would say to his son or how to comfort him. After a few moments of quiet settling, I asked him to feel into his distress and share his experience. He immediately blurted with tears, "I'm so ashamed we have a dark-skinned child. Life is so hard for him!" The internalized oppression message here is, *If he were white, we wouldn't be in this horrible mess!*

We hurt sometimes when we can't face our pain, and we also hurt when we do. The former, however, leads to more distress, and the latter leads to more relief. In my Mindful of Race training, I often begin with a face-to-face silent exercise where I offer several statements of recent racial events and ask participants to embody how the experience might be for the person in the event. For example, as they look at each other face to face in silence, I will say, "I'm Heather Heyer. I'm a white woman who showed up to protest racism in Charlottesville and was killed." I invite participants to rotate several times while I offer different examples.

In one such training with a diverse group, Maggie, a black woman, stayed after the retreat to share with me how disappointed she was that a black woman wasn't represented in that beginning exercise and how invisible her pain was once again in a sea of white people. She was being very deliberate and controlled in her feedback to me, and I could tell she had been deeply hurt by my not referencing black women specifically—a hurt she had carried through the end of the retreat. I could empathize with her pain, having felt many times the subtle ways we as black women are made invisible. After I mentally kicked my own ass a bit for making such an omission, I acknowledged the pain she had expressed, joined in it, and apologized. We were silent for a couple of breaths, and I could sense that she felt my sincerity while also honoring the hurt she was moving through. After I sensed that we had settled together, I asked, "What did you experience after I disappointed you?"

Maggie: I stopped listening. For most of the day, I didn't hear much of what you said. It was as if I were in a daze or trance.

Ruth: It sounds like you shut down.

Maggie: Yes, I shut down.

Ruth: Are you still feeling like it is necessary to shut down, to protect yourself?

Maggie: Yes.

Ruth: I know I'm asking a lot here, but are you willing to trust me in a guided inquiry?

Maggie: Yes.

Ruth: Close your eyes and take a couple of deep breaths. [Pause] Tell me what you are feeling inside right now.

Maggie: I don't want to be shut down, but it's difficult to forgive you.

Ruth: That makes sense. I have deeply disappointed you.

Maggie: Yes.

Ruth: What's the hardest part about forgiving or letting go? What belief are you holding?

Maggie: Things will never change. I will always be disappointed.

Ruth: How does it feel inside to believe that things will never change and that you will always be disappointed?

Maggie: I feel angry.

Ruth: What sensations are informing you that you are angry? What sensations are obvious in your mind and body right now?

Maggie: I feel tightness in my forehead and hard pulsing in my throat. And my ears are burning.

Ruth: Just allow those sensations to be there without resistance, and tell me when they cool or subside.

A couple of minutes passed.

Ruth: What's happening now?

Maggie: The tightness and pulsing have softened.

Ruth: The tightness and pulsing have softened. Things have changed.

Maggie: Yes, it changed. I'm enjoying the softening in my head, throat, and chest. It feels warm.

Ruth: Yes, softening, warmth. Continue to allow that to be known.

A couple of minutes passed. She physically appeared softer. Her entire body appeared to be breathing.

Ruth: You may open your eyes.

We rested in the quiet between us for several seconds.

Ruth: Thank you for trusting my care. Know how deeply sorry I am for disappointing you. Be kind to yourself during this tender time. Rest in the softness you are experiencing, in the letting go that is naturally happening. Know you can weather the storm of disappointment and grow well, warm, and wise from it. We are brave in our care for each other.

It is this rupture, the heartbreak—this thing that happens right after the aggression or assault to the soul—that we want to attend to tenderly. It is inevitable that we will get our hearts broken again and again; we cannot control that. But we also can't stop there. What needs our care in such moments is the heartbreak itself—that crippling, crumpling, shutting down that occurs, that closing of the heart, that necessary hiding. When we care for that territory together, we are beginning to heal. Such caring is a mindfulness practice.

Having been in such circumstances many times, I have faith in our ability to recover. It may not always be as quickly as we would like, but most of us have the capacity to recover. And we can help each other to do this. We can move through our hurt together by shifting into mindfulness and away from fixation on who or what is wrong. What supports recovery in such moments is to turn inward toward the bruising and to care tenderly for the hurt we are experiencing.

To shift the entrenched programing of internalized oppression, POC are challenged to go against the stream—to reach out and know the full body of color more intimately within our racial identity groups and across racial identity groups. We need not assume solidarity; rather, we need to discover and admire our beauty in wonderment and awe. When we incline our hearts in this direction, we are in the practice of "golden repair."

Anger Is Not Transformative—It's Initiatory

I imagine that one of the reasons that people cling to their hate and prejudice so stubbornly is because they sense that once hate is gone, they will be forced to deal with their own pain.
JAMES BALDWIN

Anger, whether expressed or silenced, is no stranger to many POC. When we are in the heat of it, it's hard to be mindful of anything else, including the teachings in this book. But the good thing about anger is that it gets our attention! Once it has our attention, how we relate to it is vitally important. Anger first lives in the mind; therefore, we must examine our mind, especially our beliefs, and notice if anger is leading to more distress or to its release.

In my first book, *Healing Rage: Women Making Inner Peace Possible*, I shared a time when I was in therapy. For several weeks, I would rant and rage about the white people on the job—how ignorant they were, how it was necessary for me to point out their blindness, how they didn't like it and didn't listen but would instead toss me aside and use their power to isolate me, how defeated I felt, and how it never seemed to end. For weeks, my therapist would sit in quiet support, mainly because there wasn't room for her to add a word. I took up all the space, splattering hate and blame all over the walls. She eventually somehow managed to simply say, "Why do you send her to the job?" I was stumped by this question and asked, "What do you mean, why do I send her to the job?" She replied, "Why do you send the raging one—the one that keeps getting defeated? Why don't you send the wise one? She would probably do a better job!"

What was staggering about that moment is that it never occurred to me that I had any other choice. I only knew one part of me—the rager. I also believed that my freedom from the distress I was experiencing was solely dependent on white people changing—either getting what I was saying or, better yet, agreeing with me. Little did I know, this was delusional thinking.

Why are we, as POC, so shocked when racial ignorance and injustice rears its ugly head? Why does it send us into a rage? Often, our responses are a mix of aversion, delusion, and trauma. Our aversion is because we hate what is happening with a passion. Our delusion is that, even though we acknowledge that we live in a racialized society, we assume racism should not show its face. When it does, we are shocked out of delusion into our senses. But then we don't stay in our senses—we go to war. We continue to talk about the shock of it. And the "shock of it" is often rooted in trauma.

What's unresolved from the past gets activated, and our nervous system goes into overload. We feel threatened and feel that we must either fight or take flight, both of which make the present inaccessible. In our reactivity, we vacate the premises of our own body and heart, just when our mind needs them most.

After realizing that I was more than my anger, I brought this curiosity to my mindfulness practice. I began to notice, for example, how much I suffered when I was angry, what I avoided when I was angry, and my unexamined and subtler belief that *vulnerability* and *weakness* were synonyms as opposed to distinct experiences. I also realized that I could not hate my way out of the messes I got myself into. As I stepped more honestly into being angry and tasted the suffering I was experiencing,

I discovered a new and subtler kind of freedom: I gradually noticed that I could sit with my feelings with less anxiety and without acting on them, and I could use the light of anger to look deeper and use its warmth to heal.

It is not uncommon for me to meet POC who are in deep distress and outrage over racial ignorance and injustice. Often, this anger is coupled with activism. The focus is so collected around white people and institutional harm that POC are unaware of how much they themselves are hurting and hurting others. Of course we are angry about the senseless harm so many are experiencing, and it must be stopped. But we must question the quality of our resistance. Anger may get us what we want temporarily, but resistance rooted in hate blocks the arteries we need for heart balance and flow. Imagine putting effort in and leaving hate out.

We must ask ourselves, "In what ways do I use anger to feel more alive or more courageous? Is anger the best (or only) way I know how to connect with other POC? Can I know anger without hating? What is my relationship with tenderness? Who am I without struggle? Who are we together as POC without a common enemy?" Such questions are not problems to be solved. They are questions that apprentice us—that bring us into moral alignment and inner harmony. Be curious and lighthearted about this inquiry. We are looking at our relationship to the questions more than driving to answer them.

All of life is habit, and we can change. Through mindfulness, we can interrupt and transform the repetitive motion injury of anger. Working with anger is best done when you are not activated or in the middle of a crisis, but rather when you can reflect in an atmosphere of self-compassion. Begin to explore these questions both in your sitting practice with RAIN discussed in chapter 10 and in your RAGs. Incorporate the practices of kindness and compassion to support this inquiry.

Bid or Pass: A Call to Balance

I grew up playing a card game called bid whist, popular among African Americans. Four people play this game, representing two pairs. The cards are dealt face down and six cards are placed in a pile called the kitty. After a review of what has been dealt to you and a wild guess after reading the face of your partner, you either bid or pass on the kitty. You bid when you think you can win the game and that your partner and/or the kitty will somehow have the cards you don't have. You pass when the cards dealt to you don't look promising for a win. Sometimes, when you pass, your partner will bid, and between the two of you and the kitty, you win or lose. And sometimes you discover you can pass and still win by playing the cards you were dealt in a smart way.

This strategy applies to our relationship to racial distress. You are dealt a situation face down that you can't ignore. Your partner (and the kitty) in this game is uncertainty, and your opponent is injustice. After looking at your cards, you must determine what action you will take. But here is the crucial turning point: you must decide, because even when you don't make a choice, you are making a choice.

It is wholesome to be discerning. I acknowledge that using a card-game metaphor may be too casual for the seriousness of race and racism, but hang with me for a few more pages. What I am basically attempting to illustrate is that we can't bid every hand we are dealt—we can't confront every injustice or address every need—and still stay in balance or in the game.

I once coached a high-profile, forty-two-year-old black woman in corporate America who had been put on several committees to represent the company's diversity initiative. She felt this was important work and, given her position, that she was the only one who could and should do it. This diversity work was in addition to her demanding job, which included international travel and being away from her husband and two young children. She asked me to support her with balance, which was challenging, as she repeatedly rescheduled our coaching sessions. When we did meet, she was often distracted and anxious about what she had not taken care of. She wanted support, but she didn't see how it could fit in with her other demands.

On one chilly morning, I received a call from her assistant with the news that my client had had a massive stroke. When I visited her in the hospital, she could not speak, but I could see in her eyes that her cry for recovery was as demanding as her cry of regret. Family and friends surrounded her with love and care but she never recovered. She passed away five days later.

I was quite disturbed for several weeks. This loss represented a constellation, not a star—not a single incident. Whether it's social activism or raising a family, too many of us are harming ourselves. Our habits of mind are often out of proportion to what our body and heart need or can handle. We must be more honest with ourselves and not let our ego deceive us into believing that we can be all things to all people.

CHOOSING TO BID

As POC, we are dealt unlimited opportunities to challenge racial inequity and harm. For example, if you are having a conflict with a friend or colleague and you want to maintain, or even deepen, the relationship, you bid. You may want to intervene at the individual level and speak directly to the conflict between you. Using the "talking about what disturbs you" guideline (see chapter 14) could be useful to apply in such situations.

There are times when you will want to address the group-identity level and speak to the dominant and subordinated racial dynamics that feed oppression. In such instances, it's not solely about you or your feelings, nor is it about what an individual is doing. You are speaking as a racial group member to another racial group or member, and you are acknowledging racial group behavior and patterns of harm. In such situations, you can apply the "six hindrances to racial harmony" (see chapter 4) as your bid.

Then there are situations that warrant institutional intervention—when individuals or racial groups come together to form a movement or join a cause that addresses systemic and structural racism. Black Lives Matter, MoveOn.org, Indivisible, and the Love Army are some recent examples. We bid when we join groups to support others, share resources, oppose policies and practices that cause racial harm, and propose practices that foster social equity and well-being.

The word *bid* might feel strange or a bit too quirky, but consider this: *bid* is another word for choosing, saying "yes," or saying "hell no." Your partner is uncertainty; you are not in complete control of the outcome, and you are playing to transform racial obstacles—your opponents. To bid is to be open to learning how to play the game more skillfully. You may not always win the game but will inevitably become more aware and become a better player.

CHOOSING TO PASS

Too many of us are out of balance. We overextend without realizing that we live in a body, ignoring the call to be nourished and nurtured. We must find time to rest from our wounding and from clear seeing, to reflect, and to heal. Yet many POC I speak to feel as though it is a luxury to take a break from the challenges in their lives. Resting is not a betrayal; it is a restorative necessity.

To come into balance is to learn how to pass. We pass when we choose to withdraw effort—to not expend energy outward, to not be on hyper alert twenty-four/seven, and to bring ourselves into balance through a devotion to self-care.

Often, to pass means you learn to rely on your bid-whist partner—uncertainty—to carry more of the weight for a while. This requires that you develop a more intimate relationship with uncertainty and with ease.

There are many ways to contemplate a relationship with these mind states. Most spiritual traditions have practices that support such well-being, such as prayer, inspirational readings, songs, wise teachings, or dance. Explore practices that bring you into balance and that support you in strengthening inner resources of well-being.

I encourage POC to attend a Vipassana or insight meditation retreat at least once a year. Within a ten-day retreat structure, through periods of silence, sitting, and walking meditation, we are supported in slowing down and noticing the workings of our heart and mind. We begin to see more clearly the nature of mind, and we experience more inner stability, confidence, and well-being. With practice, we begin to notice increasing moments of release from distress and how freedom is not a destination outside of our own mental creation.

An insight meditation retreat fuels moral reflection. It strengthens our capacity to examine personal and cultural habits of mind and what it is like to release them. It reveals a gradual and natural unveiling of the truth of suffering, and it further supports us in cultivating a heart we can learn to trust and rest in. Knowing these experiences directly is restorative and brings balance to our lives.

When I encourage POC to attend an insight meditation retreat, it is often difficult for them to pause and embrace the idea or to take the time. But rarely is it a waste of time. Many insight retreats are offered freely, while other retreat centers provide scholarship support. As one participant of color shared, "Meditation helps to keep my mind in the present and not ruminate about my past. It helps to calm my mind from obsessive thinking, which leads to anxiety. I'm currently learning how to cope and grieve my current circumstances while still working on gratitude and self-love."

As POC, it is essential that we know the taste of freedom and pursue it. An African American woman shyly approached me at the end of a ten-day retreat. Her voice was soft when she whispered, "Is it okay to be happy?" Her eyes smiled, and her face was radiant. She said, "In this moment, I'm happier than I have ever been! Is it really okay to allow it?" She was not really looking for an answer, just a witness—a face that looked like hers. We just smiled together, enjoying happiness together, as we looked caringly into each other's eyes. Insight meditation retreats are one way for us to answer our deepest questions, even the ones that have no answers.

Another way to "pass" is to retreat with each other. Self-organizing a retreat allows us to share our diverse experiences, traditions, and ceremonies and to talk to each other about what hurts and what heals. Too many of us are afraid of looking weak or vulnerable or of being disappointed or feeling unworthy. We worry that in asking for help we are taxing an overtaxed community with one more burden. Such beliefs need to be tested. I know many POC who have received more care than they can bear. In fact, they discovered that although asking for support was difficult, what was more difficult was receiving it. There is much talent among us. Allowing ourselves to be cared for is a practice we can learn to do well. We need not be ashamed of being human.

In exploring how we use our energy—whether we bid or pass—we discover that it is not about either/or; rather it is about both/and. We need balance—self-care *and* engagement. It is a win-win practice.

Talk to Children about
Tenderness and Strength

One characteristic of being socially subordinated is that many POC groups talk about race. Conversations may be prideful or laced with fear and outrage against a common enemy—often, white individuals and white supremacy. Whether prideful or outraged, such talks do not always deal authentically with the vulnerability that lies underneath such emotions or the tenderness required for a family or community to recover together.

In my family, we were taught to be strong, to stand up and fight against racial injustice. We would be sent back to finish a fight if it was learned that we had left cowardly or were defeated. If we won the fight, we felt justified to boast, but rarely was the bruising we felt from the physical and mental blows attended to. We could talk about the racial other to each other, but we could not speak of the vulnerability of being a racial other to each other. Tenderness was considered a threat we could not afford. Collectively, we see the effects of such unattended vulnerabilities manifesting as hypertension, high blood pressure, inflammatory diseases, addictions, depression, and autoimmune diseases, to name a few.

Claire, a Cuban woman in the Mindful of Race training, spoke of her concern for her sixteen-year-old daughter who had an eating disorder. Her appearance was flawless and efficient, her voice controlled, and her speech fast-paced.

Ruth: When did you first notice the symptoms of your daughter's eating disorder?

Claire: When my daughter was twelve, a nineteen-year-old white guy attacked her on her way home from school. It was an attempted rape, but she fought him off. The doctor took an X-ray, gave her a neck brace and pain pills, and sent us home. She was okay. We got through it. I believe the eating problem began within months after that incident, but I can't be sure.

Ruth: What a horrific incident for her, you, and the family. How did you and your daughter attend to the emotional trauma of that occurrence?

Claire: We made sure the guy was arrested. Her brother walked her to and from school each day, and we enrolled her in self-defense classes.

Ruth: These are important things for her protection and the protection of others. And how was the emotional trauma attended to? Did you talk about the pain of this horror together?

Claire: No, we have not done that.

This was true with Claire and her daughter, and it continues to be true with members of my own family of origin. The "true" I am speaking to is this tendency we have as POC to "not go there"—to not talk to each other in tender ways about the emotional traumas of being a race.

Such living trauma is not uncommon among communities of color. Most African American parents I talk to share with me the terror they experience every time their children are out of their sight, regardless of the age of their children! For many of us, the terror is spoken of, but the tenderness, which I am convinced is deeply felt, is left unvoiced. Learning to speak openly and tenderly about race to our children is a mindfulness practice that supports us in coming out of hiding.

What stories, knowingly or unknowingly, do we tell our children and dear ones about race? Are they truthful? Do they instill fear, hope, anger, shame, defeat, or pride? What's left out? Unknown? Forbidden? What story would humanize and harmonize your relationship with dear ones?

An example of such a story is told by national correspondent for the *Atlantic*, Ta-Nehisi Coates. In his book *Between the World and Me*, he writes to his son, sharing intimate stories about what it's like living in a black body. He shares, "Your mother had to teach me how to love you—how to kiss you and tell you that I loved you every night." He then describes his first trip out of the country to Paris, a trip made at the insistence of his wife:

> A few weeks into our stay, I made a friend who wanted to improve his English as much as I wanted to improve my French. We met one day out in the crowd in front of Notre Dame. We walked to the Latin Quarter. We walked to a wine shop. Outside the wine shop there was seating. We sat and drank a bottle of red. We were served heaping piles of meats, bread, and cheese. Was this dinner? Did people do this? I had not even known how to imagine it. And more, was this all some elaborate ritual to get an angle on me?
>
> My friend paid. I thanked him. But when we left I made sure he walked out first. He wanted to show me one of those old buildings that seem to be around every corner in that city. And the entire time he was leading me, I was sure he was going to make a quick turn into an alley, where some dudes would be waiting to strip me of . . . what, exactly?
>
> But my new friend simply showed me the building, shook my hand, gave a fine "high five" and walked

off into the wide-open night. And watching him walk away, I felt that I had missed part of the experience because of my eyes—because my eyes were made in Baltimore; because my eyes were blindfolded by fear. Even in Paris, I could not shake the old ways, the instinct to watch my back at every pass, and always be ready to run.

This story and others like them, like James Baldwin's *The Fire Next Time*, offer tenderness and racial insight. They also offer a way out—something all children need, near and far—a way to see clearly how we can bring understanding and emotional wisdom to racial distress. Every child of color should bathe in the rich, racial clarity and wisdom of such writers and members of our community.

As a person of color, what might you tell your children or other children of color about racial truth and healing? Without judgment, allow yourself to experience whatever you are noticing in your body, mind, and heart as you consider making this offer. If telling your children the truth about racism feels too difficult, explore what's difficult about it. For example, are you too angry to be clear? Do you feel depressed or helpless? Do you fear they won't listen or hear you? Explore as tenderly as possible what gets in the way of talking out loud about race and racism to the children in a healing way.

When sharing stories, it is helpful to know your racial inheritance and history. For example, what unfinished business did you inherit from your parents or ancestors? What racial stories need to be aired, honored, or even questioned?

I was raised with the story that my grandfather, whom I never met, was half American Indian of the Choctaw Nation of Mississippi. I was told that my grandfather met my grandmother when her family was under his reservation's protection as they fled the South to move west in the 1920s. However, in 2017, through Ancestry.com, the results, to my surprise, showed that my roots were 70 percent African (mostly Ivory Coast, Ghana, and Nigeria), 29 percent European (mostly England, Scotland, and Wales), and less than 1 percent Native American. It's hard to know what's absolutely true given that DNA strands for American Indians are not well researched, but it sure made my head spin to hear that, according to this text, I was more European than Native American. And then I mused, *If it turns out we are all racial mutts, would that shift the racial narrative?* It would, at a minimum, give us entertaining tales.

Storytelling is a healing art form, and we all have many stories to tell and many to listen and open to. Stories that are both tender and wise keep our hearts well lubricated and our ears attuned to humility and care. And it is an artful way to plant seeds that help us wake up, remember our belonging, and serve well. In her book *God Help the Child*, Toni Morrison describes a family dinner ritual of asking two questions: (1) What have you learned that's true, and how do you know it's true? And, (2) What problems do you have? Imagine this as an evening ritual with the children and other dear ones. Then hold them and look at them as if they hung the moon!

Envision Life Beyond Struggle

Two examples stay with me that point to our need to have a vision larger than struggle. On a trip to South Africa shortly after Nelson Mandela was elected president, I met with dozens of nongovernmental organization leaders to both share in the exuberance of this achievement and to hear thoughts on moving forward. One of the questions I asked was, "What now?" Most of the people I met with were stunned by the question. Their families, having fought against apartheid for generations, had not given thought to envisioning a life beyond struggle. The second example was when I offered a keynote address on generational healing at the Association of Black Psychologists' annual convention. I asked, "Who are you in the absence of racial suffering?" One woman responded straightway, "I would lose a big part of my identity. I would feel rather empty." These two examples were stunningly sobering and reminded me of the question W. E. B. Dubois asked, "If your color faded or the color line . . . was miraculously forgotten . . . , what is it that you would want? What would you immediately seek?"

The violence that structural racism inflicts on the psyche of dark bodies has, over generations, impacted our natural impulse to envision the future. We are hardwired to see what's wrong and to fight against it. Yet, we also need to imagine our lives beyond struggle and have a vision that is larger than resistance or war.

Spend some time with dear ones, perhaps in your RAG, and imagine humanity without racial suffering or injury. What do you see? How does it feel? What would institutions, politicians, leaders, or unafraid people be doing differently? What would the elders, helpers, and children be doing? What would need to start, stop, or continue for this vision of racial well-being to manifest? As you envision this, is what you see tasteable, touchable, good for all, and achievable? How does this vision nourish future generations? What role do you play in making this happen?

Make crafting your vision a mindfulness practice. Write it down and refine it as needed. It may take several months to fine-tune your vision, and it's okay to continue refining it. Once you have a solid paragraph or page, give this vision center stage in your life and use it as a pointer for aligning your actions with your intentions.

Concluding Thoughts

These suggestions only begin to touch the vast surface of complexity that represents our lives. They are meant to inspire contemplation and hope for our well-being as a body of color. Be creative and create more inquires to heal as a body of color.

17

Artistry

Cultural Medicine

Suffering leads us to beauty the way thirst leads us to water.

JANE HIRSHFIELD, Soto Zen practitioner

Art is the community's medicine for the worst disease of mind, the corruption of consciousness.

ROBIN G. COLLINGWOOD, *The Principles of Art*

As we become more mindful and begin to acknowledge the prolonged, persistent, and spiritual thievery of racial suffering and injustice, the energy we need to serve and reunite the world becomes available to us. We can use this energy creatively—not just for ourselves, but to serve and heal a larger heart as well. Expressing ourselves artistically supports us in realizing freedom and generosity.

For me, writing has never been easy, but neither has it been an option. When I was writing my first book, *Healing Rage*, I remember meeting with elder, author, and cultural anthropologist Angeles Arrien. I had just left my corporate job and was devoting myself to writing and spiritual practice. I wanted to talk about my struggles, but what I really wanted was to rest in her kind, quiet, wise presence. We had tea together, and she offered two cookies of sage advice. First, she told me to tell the truth in kind ways, and second, she said that when writing is a struggle, remember to do something that brings you joy, like dancing, listening to music, or gardening. I've been writing and dancing ever since! I love breaking out into an instantaneous, goofy-like dance for no good reason then laughing myself into lightness. Somehow it creates more inner space, and I'm reminded that I don't have to work so hard.

There is a relationship between suffering and beauty. That's why we have stories like *Beauty and the Beast* and *King Kong*. That's why roses have thorns, we make lemonade out of lemons, and the lotus flower blooms in mud. Art is the language of kinship—an attempt to make sense out of suffering. As Jane Hirshfield, Soto Zen practitioner and poet, shares:

> We make art . . . partly because our lives are ungraspable, uncarryable, impossible to navigate without it. . . . Art isn't a superficial addition to our lives; it's as necessary as oxygen. . . . Art allows us to find a way to agree to suffering, to include it and not be broken, to say *yes* to what actually is, and then to say something further, something that changes and opens the heart, the ears, the eyes, the mind. . . . A work of art is always a conversation, not a monologue.

We all desire to be unique in a world of seven billion people. When the spider builds its web, the web is a mirror image of itself—a beauty we are more likely to pause and admire even if we are afraid of spiders. We are awestruck and wonder, *How is this possible?* Like the spider, our unique expression is something we must realize and reveal as it reflects our sole signature, our thumbprint, our web that connects us to all things. Everybody has a story to tell—a question in search of an answer, an itch in search of a scratch, something that once revealed would shock you, surprise you, depress you, enlighten you, and inspire you. No one can perfect this gift but you, and no one else can express it the way you do. Perfection here is of the highest standard—your own. It is a moving standard not to be met but to aspire to. Consider art medicine for the heart.

Art carries its own emotional intelligence and power. It helps us understand and experience the world directly and abstractly. Art fortifies, enlivens, and brightens culture. It can reshape our perceptions and stimulate curiosity in humanity. We create to understand something, to figure something out, to know something more intimately and more deeply, or to say something. To express oneself in art is to explore and even dissolve the edges of the ordinary; to penetrate resistance and tumble into mystery itself and be carried by it. It feels like a personal journey, but I believe it is the revelation of something deeply needed—in fact, something that belongs to all of us.

One of my fondest childhood memories was peeking out the bedroom door on the third Friday night of each month, when we had improvisational jazz jam sessions at our house. I was around ten years old, and my younger sisters and I couldn't come out of our room. But we could peek, and, lucky for us, music has no boundaries.

Because my mother played the piano, the most stationary instrument, all the other musicians had to bring their instruments to our home. I remember them piling into the living room—the bass fiddle, saxophones, trumpets, drums. There was a full range of African and Afro-Cuban percussions and singers, representing diverse races but mostly African Americans; they included business owners, politicians, the working poor, and the unemployed. It was in the late 1950s, the start of the civil rights movement, when many of the musicians, including my mom, were actively involved with the National Association for the Advancement of Colored People (NAACP). Our communities were endangered, and close members of our family had been threatened, imprisoned, and regularly harassed by the police.

And then there was jazz. My mother was fully in her power when she played the piano. I would watch her in awe. She would start the preliminary rhythm, and then everyone else would join in at random times based on what they were hearing and what they felt would add value, meaning, interest, and harmony. They were playing for each other, and there was deep respect and trust in what was unfolding. No one contributed just to be heard but rather to create something more beautiful than what was heard and felt. I remember how my mom would often hum a rhythm before expressing it on the piano. This would go on for some time, and when I would finally hear it in concert with the other musicians, I was amazed at how it was strengthened and vitalized by the grace of their ears and hearts and union. There was a sense of complementarity, not competition, as if they knew they were in co-creation and that something subtle and mysterious was unfolding. The sounds each musician made were like statements and questions that the other musicians were affirming and answering, the very meaning of which was expanded and changed in response.

Every musician and singer was highlighted at a certain time, but it was never truly a solo. It was more spacious and spontaneous—an inflection, gradation, unassuming yet distinct, a fragrance. Most of them could play music much better than they could speak, and they preferred it that way. No one had sheet music, and no one followed a script. The ears and heart were in charge. It was the listening and the emotion absent of words or reason that was on display. No one could make what was happening happen on their own. What they created together could not be repeated, and it wasn't meant to be. It was a gift in the moment—a gift that did not require words. In fact, it was a gift that spoke louder than words—a gift of presence, genuine expression, exchange, and care. The musicians themselves were nourished and fortified, and everyone in their range was touched. I felt my body dissolve into sound and become sound without separation. I had no words at the time that could explain the joy I felt experiencing the deep love they were creating and sharing. These same musicians would be in church on Sunday morning, sharing their gifts with the congregation.

The idea of deep listening, waiting in stillness, adding value, changing direction, harmonizing, and ears and hearts moving body parts struck a wordless cord in my heart at an early age—and it continues to do so to this day. It reminds me of a simple but profound sentence that Toni Morrison used in her book *God Help the Child*: "Silence is as close to music as you can get." She must have known my heart.

This early experience spoke of sensitivity, attunement, respect, and recognition of our sound in a larger soundtrack. It spoke to our capacity to unify, transform, and heal. And it reflected unimaginable beauty and exquisite truth. Little did I know that this early impression would become a creative metaphor for cultural care.

To express ourselves artistically is a mindfulness practice in that we are inescapably both creator and that which is being created. As we courageously give ourselves to our artistic expression, we cultivate patience, empathy, discipline, and our capacity to hold energy as it cooks and simmers into an offering of truth to ourselves and a caring offering to our culture. It's not always simple; it puts us into the direct realization that life is not personal, permanent, or perfect. Jazz bassist Charles Mingus said it this way: "In my music, I'm trying to play the truth of what I am. The reason it's difficult is because I'm changing all the time."

Art speaks to a truth larger than our suffering, and our job is to make a genuine offer. Whether you are a writer, dancer, healer, sculptor, painter, singer, architect, teacher, gardener, philosopher, or caregiver, your offering is sure to be medicine for collective well-being.

Consider your life a gift. What's inside? What creative expressions are you warehousing that bring you alive and belong to all of us? Philosopher, theologian, and civil rights leader Howard Thurman encouraged us in this way: "Don't ask yourself what the world needs. Ask yourself what makes you come alive and then go do that. Because what the world needs is people who have come alive."

Imagination has enormous power and can create the future. What beauty have you always wanted to express? Do you long to create a play? Write a poem? Sing jazz? Play the drums? Dance like wildfire? These art forms, and many others like them, are prayers that allow everything we are on the inside to come out.

Identify a creative project—something your heart is curious about that you might enjoy. Consider your artistic expression, no matter how large or small, a gesture of affection that cultivates a culture of care. Offer it generously, as ceremony, and without apology. Pay attention to how you and others are impacted.

The offerings of our creativity are noble and emancipating. When practiced, we come out of hiding into light. When shared, it supports love and respect and inspires harmony and hope. It's a gesture of gratitude, a way of giving back. To say yes to our artistic calling is to say to our culture, *Here is my offering of care.*

Maybe the word *artist* feels a bit far-fetched to you. If this is the case, make whatever you do—the simple and profound—ceremonies of love with prayers of well-being.

18

Equanimity Practice

Out beyond ideas of wrongdoing and rightdoing,
there is a field. I'll meet you there. When the soul lies down in
that grass, the world is too full to talk about. Ideas, language,
even the phrase each other *doesn't make any sense.*

RUMI

I often think of our power and how quickly things can change with a caring and wise heart. I think of those times when we see beyond judgment and self-interest and realize that we are choosing instead of reacting; those times when racial distress is held in our hearts, while the mind is still, steady, and clear; those times when we make small choices that show great care and influence social balance. This is the power of equanimity.

Equanimity is often depicted in images of stillness, ease, compassion, and strength. In Buddhism, equanimity is prominent, often referenced as a crowning mind state or the fruit of spiritual practice. It means to stand in the middle of all things. I'm told that a common reference to equanimity in India is "to see with patience." It is a sustained state of balance, seeing what's here with evenness of mind—a mind that is touched by life but unbroken by its ever-changing nature.

Equanimity is an invaluable inner resource that is cultivated through awareness. It is the experience of knowing the energetic movements of mind without reactivity. It is an experience of grounded presence in the midst of extremes, when the mind is steady and responsive, and when we can say to ourselves,

"This moment is like this, and it doesn't have to be different right now. I can allow what is here and offer what is needed." Imagine the power of this inner resource as we move through a racialized world.

Several years ago, as I boarded a plane in South Africa for the long flight back to California, I looked forward to taking a long-needed nap in a totally booked plane. Finally, on board and in the air, I rested further into my seat and pushed the button to recline. The person seated behind me, a white male, began to slam his food tray, which was on the back of my seat, up and down repeatedly, making sure I felt it. Initially, I was annoyed and ignored it, but when it continued, grumbles included, and I could feel a sense of hostility, I turned and quietly asked, "Would you be willing to stop slamming your food tray up and down on the back of my seat?" To which he yelled—and I do mean yelled, "If you hadn't leaned your chair back into my lap, it wouldn't be necessary."

A flash of silence shot through the plane while a flood of thoughts rattled my mind: *Who in hell does this white fool think he's talking to? I have a right to recline my chair. How dare you disrespect a black woman, and so publicly. You wouldn't treat a white man this way.* I was furious and felt chastised and embarrassed. I could also sense how others on the plane had been triggered by his response. It appeared as though the flight attendants had gone AWOL, several people started fidgeting and coughing, the white men opened newspapers as if on cue, babies started crying, black men began to unbuckle their seat belts and stand up. My mind heard a white woman asking if someone could open a window, and the black women were staring at me, rolling their heads as if to say, "I hope you kick his ass so I don't have to!" It was quite the "deer in the headlights" moment—all of it taking place within ninety seconds.

What do you imagine I did?

While this incident wasn't overtly about race, racial distress had been activated, and, in addition to my own distress, it needed to be attended to. I could have gone to war, insisting on my right to recline my seat, but there was more at play than my comfort. The white man seated behind me could have handled the situation more skillfully and less hatefully, but he didn't. What was happening wasn't personal or permanent, and it was far from perfect. We were thirty thousand feet in the air for the next twelve hours. I considered my height, being short enough not to be severely impacted by a reclined seat—it was my right and preference, not a necessity. I was at a choice point.

I raised my seat.

When I raised my seat, the plane body distress settled and came into balance. I'm not suggesting that I was not rattled by the white man's verbal assault. But I did not become unglued nor was I knocked off center—I could be with what was happening while it was happening and attune to the collective nervous system of the enclosed plane without feeling severely compromised. Deep within me, I was okay.

An hour or so later, when I stood to stretch my legs, I looked at the white man sitting behind me. He had fallen asleep. I noticed the peace in his face, and I also noticed that he was close to seven feet tall. His knees more than touched the back of my seat, and I could see how reclining my chair created a hardship for him. I imagined how often he had been teased as a child for being tall and awkward, and I wondered how long he had had this attitude and how he may have felt "put upon" or even bullied by others. Seeing such innocence softened the hard edge of the ignorance he had displayed earlier. This was followed by intense soreness in my chest as I recognized walking through the tight aisles of the plane that most of the people I passed were white men. I realized that there was a secret wish that flashed through me—a wish for a white ally; someone who would have intervened and said something like: Man that was rude. You owe this woman an apology. Yet within this soreness, and from years of mindfulness practice, I knew that my freedom and well-being was not dependent on anyone's behavior going my way. In that moment, I just gave my heart caring rubs.

Equanimity is awareness so spacious that whatever arises in our mind and heart, whether agreeable or disagreeable, is small and incidental compared to awareness itself. In other words, when we are equanimous, nothing is left out of heart's view.

We might begin to understand equanimity using nature as a metaphor. For example, equanimity can feel internally like a great mountain, with the mind solid and stable, undisturbed by the changing seasons. Or it can be like the ocean, with the mind vast, deep, and immeasurable, undisturbed by whatever swims, floats, or is housed in its waters. Equanimity can be like a strong fire—roaring, engulfing, and transmuting, undisturbed by whatever is thrown into it. Or like immense space—open, allowing, and receiving, undisturbed by the objects that arise and pass away.

As we walk through the minefields of social injustice and hardship, we may want to call on the strength of these elemental inner resources for balance and equipoise. For example, there are times when we will need to stand our ground, strong like a mountain, and observe what emerges, or we may need to add a spark of fiery truth to a situation. Other times, we may need to open and allow more space around the tightness of our worries, or let go and be held by an ocean of love. As I reflect on the plane incident, I can see how I relied on the element of space to open to everyone on the plane, not just my own right or comfort and to not let my thoughts morph into war. In this choice, the entire nervous system of the plane came into balance as I did. Play with this imagery until it feels like a natural and accessible inner resource.

Many civil rights movements that push against systemic oppression are driven by fierce compassion and the need for social balance—social equanimity. One fine example is the Standing Rock water protectors, organized around an indigenous template from Lakota values, showing us how to wisely think about collective and poised resistance. They continue to demonstrate care for our interconnectivity, compassion for all, and harmlessness.

Another example is the Black Lives Matter movement. In an atmosphere of intense hatred toward black bodies, Black Lives Matter works across a broad spectrum in which black lives are being systematically and intentionally targeted for disgrace and demise. This work includes resistance to state violence toward black people living in poverty, US and undocumented immigrants, black incarceration, and exploitation of black girls and black people who are differently abled, as well as the relentless assault on black women, girls, queer, and trans people. Black Lives Matter is a national resistance movement that affirms black humanity and resilience and strives for liberation.

These are just two examples of spiritual activism that seek social equanimity—balance that relieves the stress of humanity.

The cultivation of equanimity begins on the inside. Actually, it is more like a returning to an inner strength core to our existence but forgotten. In the early 1980s, well before becoming a mindfulness practitioner, while living in Santa Cruz, California, I had a dream. I saw myself with a round body sitting on a budding flower in the middle of a still lake. The sun was shining bright, and the birds were singing my favorite song, yet there was a torrential storm hammering down on my body. Chiseled on the hail and lightning were partial faces and body parts of people I had been in conflict with, yet I only felt clarity, contentment, and ease. I awoke from the dream, but I never forgot the potency of poise in the midst of horrendous conflict or that prevailing experience of profound neutrality, evenness, and balance of mind—undisturbed by the storm. Not only did I taste the promise of equanimity, I also pursued it. It would be another decade before I came to understand the symbolism of this dream; the fat, content body with my face was my Buddha nature, my capacity to awaken, sitting on the flowering lotus—the flower of becoming—having a peaceful war with Mara, the deity of desire and temptation.

Equanimity is not something we can force. It's an experience we come to recognize and nurture through mindfulness practice. As we taste and rest in the inner tranquility that is the character of equanimity, we become, through our lived example, an energetic resource contributing to a culture of care.

Equanimity invites us to be aware with balanced and wise effort. Like a violin that can't offer the right sound if the strings are too tight or too loose, so is true in the body and mind. We attune or fine-tune our inner strings by taking a posture that supports balance. Meditation teacher and fiction writer Lila Kate Wheeler inspired the phrases used in the following practice.

Guided Equanimity Practice

For this practice, sit up a little higher than usual, but without tension, and begin to move your awareness through your body to invite relaxation. Rest in your intention to be at ease, peaceful.

Begin to inquire, *What am I aware of? What's obvious?*

Take your time. Notice if the effort you are making is agitating the mind and heart. Continue to relax the mind in the body. Let the energy settle downward and inward as you take long, deep breaths. Tune into any feelings of calm, no matter how slight. Notice how calm and ease are felt in the body and mind.

As you settle, thoughts will arrive—that's okay. The mind thinks! That's its job, and it's shamelessly on duty twenty-four/seven. You don't make yourself think. Mind is a sense organ; it thinks. In this practice, you are choosing not to engage your thoughts; rather, you direct your attention below the surface of thought to experience how thought lives in the body.

Without effort, begin to notice the elemental quality of your awareness. Is it an experience of hardness or firmness, solid like a mountain, or are you experiencing openness or an expanse, like space? Maybe you notice a sense of inner movement or flow like the ocean or heat and warmth like fire. Keep your awareness open, without effort, without story or interpretation. Subtly attune and note the nature of your experience in this present moment. Rest and enjoy the impermanent and impersonal nature of your experiences, feeling whatever stability and balance of mind are present.

As you feel centered, reflect on one good thing you like about yourself and notice how this reflection impacts your present experience. Linger here for a while. Next, begin to repeat the following phrases quietly, feeling the phrases and the spaces in between and through them. Take your time to relax and linger in the goodwill motivating these phrases.

- May I see the world with quiet eyes.

- May I offer my care without hesitation, knowing I may be met with gratitude, anger, or resistance.

- May I find the inner resources to genuinely contribute where needed.

- May I remain peaceful and let go of fixation.

- I care about the pain of others, yet I cannot control it.

- May I offer care, knowing I don't control the course of life, suffering, or death.

- I wish all beings contentment, but I cannot make their choices for them.

- May I see my limits with compassion, just as I see the limits of others.

- May I be undisturbed by the changing circumstances of my life.

- I care for all beings, but my way is not the only way. All beings have their own journey, and I have mine.

- May I offer my support, knowing that what I offer may be of great benefit, some benefit, or even no benefit.

- May I be free from preference and prejudice.

- May I bear witness to things just as they are.

- May I offer my prayer without conditions, knowing I may be met with appreciation, resentment, and resistance.

- May I see the world with patient eyes.

Take as much time as you need repeating all or some of these phrases as often as you like, then take a few moments to rest in quiet stillness, noticing once again the elemental quality of your experience—mountain, ocean, fire, or space. Linger here until you feel ready to end your meditation with offerings of gratitude.

Concluding Thoughts

The practice of equanimity stills the mind and grounds the heart in wise understanding. It is this grounding in wisdom and compassion that fertilizes seeds of balanced well-being. Feel free to create your own equanimity phrases. If you do, understand that the phrase should not be a wish that pushes for an outcome. Rather, it is a wish that you see clearly with quiet eyes so that you can respond wisely to racial suffering and social distress. In this practice, we begin to experience alchemy—the energy we carry and offer to the world. Every thought, breath, step, and act impacts personal and social well-being. When we recognize our interdependence, we also recognize the role we play in social transformation and freedom.

Indian philosopher Jiddu Krishnamurti spoke beautifully to the essence of equanimity when he said, "When the mind is still, tranquil, not seeking any answer or solution, neither resisting or avoiding—it is only then that there can be a regeneration, because then the mind is capable of perceiving what is true; and it is the truth that liberates, not our effort to be free."

Messy at Best!

There is never time in the future in which we will work out our salvation. The challenge is in the moment; the time is always now.

JAMES BALDWIN, "Faulkner and Desegregation"

n this book, I have tried to stay close to the bones of the matter—to show the shape of racial oppression and our role in it. This book was not an attempt to resolve the racial injustice that pervades society. No book can do that. Rather it offers a framework for understanding racism and our role in it, as well as mindful strategies that reduce mental distress and increase clarity, stability, and well-being. This, in turn, supports us in responding more wisely to racial injustice, both internally and externally.

As we become more mindful, we won't be able to fit so neatly back into our small boxes. Our hearts will naturally incline toward doing what we can to co-create road maps that shift social systems, institutions, policies, and collective practices toward a more just and equitable society. We won't always know what to do or how to go about it. There is no certainty, no right way; there is only awareness and need and awkwardness. It's messy!

It's messy because too many of us pay attention to racial suffering only when we are uncomfortable, and we stop paying attention when we are comfortable again. And for those of us with good intentions, no matter how well we understand racial conditioning or how hard we try to be aware, we might still feel as if we are in hell. Being mindful of race does not guarantee comfort. It just sheds a light on what's here—this ever-changing moment.

As we bear witness to the harsh reality of race and racism and begin to heal habits of harm, we will initially be more sensitive and less confident. We are learning how to be present and more honest with ourselves, learning how to talk to others without turning away. We will feel appropriately unskilled, as though we are learning a new language. And we will discover that often being present, open to learning, and kindhearted is not only the best we can do but also all that is required in the moment.

It's messy because many of us have faced racial distress time and time again, and each time appears to be "the same old same old." And yet, each experience is exquisitely different. We can't live the same moment twice, because we are different each time. Our challenge is to discern this gradation. The meditation practices offered in this book help us de-layer our experience so we can stay present to what's here right now. This doesn't mean that history or memory is of no consequence. It means that we have agency in this moment; we can bring mindfulness to it. We can be more curious than critical, bear witness to what's here, and respond to social needs instead of react.

It's messy because racial ignorance and suffering won't be transformed in our lifetime. The racial suffering we are experiencing in the world today is the result of seeds that were planted in the past that are now blooming. We can't change the fact that those seeds were planted. Seeds have a nature: they simply blossom the racial consciousness of the past, revealing the power of our thoughts and actions. Now, with more wisdom and care, we can plant new seeds of well-being in the same soil of consciousness, which will make prior seeds of ignorance and harm more difficult to blossom. We may see such blooms in the next moment, days, or lifetimes.

It's messy because as a country, racial policies may change, but hearts tend to lag behind. The core of capitalism breeds oppression. When people are forced to do the right thing through policy, the fragrance of resentment lingers in the air, and revenge follows like a cloud. The heart must be genuinely involved to transform racism. And if hearts lag behind, there is the danger that regressive politicians will come to power and appoint regressive judges and reverse or obstruct progressive racial policies. Racism is transformed from the inside out.

It's messy because there are no clear answers that are lasting or satisfying. We discover through mindfulness practice that some questions are not meant to be answered but rather to apprentice us—they teach us to know the question more intimately, instead of driving us toward resolution. In practice, we discover that happiness and suffering are two sides of the same feather, blown by the winds of change. Neither is our enemy or our savior. Each helps us know the depth of the other. We ripen our capacity to humbly experience the nature of complexity, chaos, and uncertainty, and we know that nothing in life is personal, permanent, or perfect.

It's messy because as much as we try, we won't be mindful all the time. We will make mistakes, and we will cause harm and be harmed. It is a delusion to believe that our hearts won't be broken again and again in this awakening practice and that we won't find ourselves often in the throes of fear, righteousness, and ill will. But we can slow down, tune in, and acknowledge these contractions, forgive ourselves, and, when centered, if appropriate, apologize and forgive others.

Forgiveness is an act of compassion. We purify the heart with practice. I often advise people to pay attention to how they feel after realizing they have done something they regret; I suggest they give themselves ten "Get Out of Jail Free" cards per day. On one side of this card, they write how they blew it. On the other side, they write what they learned from it. Then they recommit to their intention to act with compassion and understanding.

Resisting forgiveness causes much injury and strengthens conceit. The wise one always forgives first. With practice, we learn how to let go. We cultivate more tenderness and discover the heart's indiscriminate and all-encompassing nature. With practice, we learn how to care without holding back, and we learn to trust that we can always begin again.

It's messy because what we do or don't do has impact—this is the interrelated truth of our existence. Understanding the basic laws of our existence affords us a beautiful opportunity to examine our experience from a wider and wiser lens and to respond to racial ignorance and suffering with an understanding of our responsibility and impact on others and future generations.

We have all been impacted by the rotten roots of racial conditioning, and we will likely not solve, in our lifetime, the social injustices and suffering that plague communities and hearts near and far. We can't choose our racial heartbreaks, but we can become more aware of how our thoughts get in the way of clear seeing, healing, and responding.

Even though this book is not about eliminating racial injustice or solving social inequities, we can be hopeful. Racial distress can be useful: it invites us to question how we live our lives. We can become more choiceful through mindfulness practice. We can stop the war within our own hearts and minds. We can cultivate more and more moments of inner freedom. We can respond to racial suffering with more clarity and wisdom. We can be more curious and aware of our impact. We can learn to forgive others and ourselves. We can live each moment in ceremony—in continuous prayer for the well-being of all races. We do this by committing ourselves to presence and reminding each other of our goodness. This is the most healing medicine of all!

In 1993, I visited southern India with a small group to study the stories of textiles, ancient health systems, and classical dance.

Our connecting flight was delayed at Cochin International Airport, so our group was put up at what appeared to be an abandoned hotel a few miles from the airport. Our flight was scheduled to leave quite early the next morning, and I and one other person in our group were the first to meet in the empty lobby. Suddenly, I heard swift movements of feet; within seconds, a sea of saffron and gold swarmed by. In the eye of that storm was His Holiness the Dalai Lama, who paused long enough to look me in the eyes with such piercing, loving presence that the next thing I knew both my friend and I were sobbing, astounded, and grateful for no good reason. To this day, his glance of compassion is palpable, reminding me of the power of loving presence—what we are all capable of with intentional practice.

Collectively we are sacred geometry, extensions of each other. We are racial beings who belong to the human race, reflecting the human heart. Imagine that our only job is to mirror each other's goodness.

Ultimately, we are beyond race. Relatively, we must deal with the harm that racial dominance and subordination produce. Each of us must ask, "What kind of society do I want to live in? How can my life be a reflection of racial harmony and an example of racial well-being for future generations?"

The end game of being mindful of race is not that we all get along or love each other because we are told it's the right thing to do. It's more about an ever-growing awareness of how we impact and care for each other. It's not a problem in my mind that we live in segregated neighborhoods or even go to separate schools, although there is much enrichment from the diversity of integration. It's more about how all neighborhoods and schools support wholesomeness and the dignity of the human spirit. It's about eliminating racial dominance and healing racial aversion. It's about ensuring that no joy is experienced at the expense of other races. It's okay that I'm not invited to your home even after knowing you for many years, but it's not okay that it's not safe for my grandchildren to leave home without the fear of being harmed and that so many brown bodies are marginalized and warehoused in prisons.

Deep within all humans is the desire to be safe, healthy, happy, and inspired and to earn a living, be respected, and be peaceful—free from harm and distress. Most POC I know are not trying to be white; they are trying to be themselves and to live without racial subordination or exploitation. All human beings, regardless of race, should have clean water, nourishing food, quality medical care, adequate shelter, and a loving sense of belonging. Too many brown and poor bodies live far removed from these basic human needs. Racial transformation requires social balance and heartfulness, where we take care of the earth and each other.

It takes more than courage not to be discouraged by racial ignorance and social injustice, but we can take strength from suffering. As Karle Wilson Baker said, "Courage is fear that has said its prayers." In this book, I have invited all of us to say our prayers, and I have given us a way to see how we got here; how we can shift from racial distress to inner freedom; and how we can heal, reach across the divide, and invest in a culture of care.

We are all habit humans—change is what we do. When we recognize and understand our racial habits of harm, we can transform them. History offers perspective and maybe a dash of hope—but don't count on hope. Count on being present and doing what must be done in the moment with as much kindness as you can imagine. To be awake is enlivening and life giving. We become more tender, less defended, more caring, and less harmful. And when we do forget to take care of each other and ourselves, we can own up, reaffirm our intention to keep our hearts open to all racial beings, and begin again.

This book was not intended to be inspirational, motivational, or even upbeat. Rather, it's a stimulus offering mature reflection that ripens our capacity to bear the truth of racial suffering more wisely—to look, feel, understand, create, and serve. Such a balanced response is hard work, necessary work, and healing work—both messy and miraculous.

The freedom we seek is not dependent on whether we can control external variables—we can't. The freedom we seek is subtler and more in our control. This freedom can be known even in a sea of ignorance and suffering. This freedom depends on us cultivating the qualities of our mind and heart so that we bring loving awareness, mindfulness, and compassion to the certainty of racial suffering and put an end to it from the inside out.

This book is just a beginning, designed for as much impact as a book can have given the limits of its pages. The rest is practice—practice that transforms racism from the inside out.

One last thing: don't be afraid of getting your heart broken. Do your work, say your prayers, then do your best. Grieve, rest, keep hate at bay, and join with others for refuge. Don't get too far ahead of now! This moment is enough to digest. Sit, breathe, open. Don't be a stranger to moments of freedom that may be flirting with you. Allow racial distress to teach you how to be more human. Sit in the heat of it until your heart is both warmed and informed, then make a conscious choice to be a light.

May we understand and transform racial habits of harm.

May we remember that we belong to each other.

May we grow in our awareness that what we do can help or hinder racial well-being.

May our thoughts and actions reflect the world
we want to live in and leave behind.

May we heal the seeds of separation inherited
from our ancestors in gratitude for this life.

May all beings, without exception,
benefit from our growing awareness.

May our thoughts and actions be
ceremonies of well-being for all races.

May we honor being diverse racial beings
among the human race, and beyond race.

May we meet the racial cries of the world with
as much wisdom and grace as we can muster.

Acknowledgments

This book represents a life's work inspired by many generations of brave ones who came before me. Deep bows of gratitude to all of my ancestors for their perseverance and love; if not for them, I wouldn't be here with such bravery and hope. I am thankful for my mother, Lodie Mae Cherry, civil rights activist and artist, who spoke the truth with persistence and without apology and who instilled in all of her children a sense of self-pride and faith. I am indebted to social justice activists and artists, past and present, who give light, love, and life in pursuit of freedom for the well-being of humanity. And I'm grateful to so many, known and unknown, who have walked beside me, often holding me up, through this book's seven-year gestation, which was both a difficult birth and a great teacher.

My understanding of transforming racism was greatly enhanced by the work of Drs. Barbara E. Riley and Delyte D. Frost of the Chambers Group LLC, who have consulted with leaders of Fortune 500 companies for over thirty-five years. Their framework, Integral Matters™: Thriving on Difference, reflected in part 1 of this book, focuses on systemic -isms, the dynamics of individuals and groups, and dominant and subordinated group behavior at all levels within organizations. I am eternally grateful to my life partner, Barbara Riley, for her wise guidance and generous support over the years, and how her work has enriched both our lives and our service to others.

I have been intravenously inspired by the fine minds and generous service of Jack Kornfield, Angela Davis, Michelle Alexander, Aishah Shahidah Simmons, Van Jones, Catherine McGee, Zenju Earthlyn Manuel, Belvie Rooks, Bryan Stevenson, Thanissara and Kittisaro, Charles Johnson, Robin

DiAngelo, Toni Morrison, Alice Walker, and Ava DuVernay, to name a few. Your strength, wisdom, and life's work have supported me in speaking freely and fearlessly.

More people than I can name have challenged my thinking and offered suggestions and inspiration along the way, including Sydney Reese, Tara Brach, Jonathan Foust, Sebene Selassie, Gil Fronsdal, Shahara Godfrey, Hugh Byrne, Robin Smith, Lauretta King, Penny Terry, DaRa Willams, Marlena deCarion, La Sarmiento, JoAnna and Andre Hardy, Nancy Ogilvie, Trudy Mitchell-Gilkey, Katie Loncke, Kate Johnson, Cheri Gardner, and Joan Lester.

I'm grateful to Barbara Riley, Ernest Cheriokee, Aubrey Pettaway, Ayofemi Oseye, Suzanne Stevens, Leora Fridman, and Shoshana Anderson for reading and providing invaluable input to various stages of the manuscript. Deep bows of gratitude to Venerable Bhikkhu Bodhi for generous and vigorous editorial support. I appreciate your wise eyes and willing hearts and that you all so clearly cared.

To those who have participated in the Mindful of Race training program over the years, thank you for showing up, for trusting me, and for teaching me. And especially to the Insight Meditation Community of Charlottesville—including Pat Coffey, Allie Rudolph, Bev Wann, Kristina Nell Weaver, and Phillip Dupont—I am grateful that you have used the Mindful of Race training to bridge community separation in Charlottesville. Thank you for your wise vision and intentional care. This book is one of many fruits of our shared labor.

A special thanks to my jewel of an agent, Laurie Fox of Linda Chester Literary Agency, for her sharp eyes and caring advocacy. Magic always happens when she is around.

While I was originally hell bent on self-publishing, this book auspiciously found its way into the loving hands of Sounds True. Producer Kriste Peoples first ignited the flame and continued to nudge by encouraging me to share a chapter or two with the Sounds True family. Meanwhile, Laurie Fox, supporting my intention to self-publish, recommended Caroline Pincus as an editor, who happened to work for Sounds True. After a quick review of a very rough draft, Caroline so believed in the book and that Sounds True should be its home that she campaigned for its acquisition and has been an extraordinary editor and passionate guide. Sounds True founder, Tami Simon, extended a warm welcome, and the talented Sounds True team has been a delight to work with. I'm in awe and grateful for this unforeseen and auspicious evolution.

Finally, I am grateful to those of you who are reading this book. I'm thankful that we are on this path together. May our light of awareness shine bright.